W9-BTE-518

Racquetball

Dedication

To my wife Sue, who provided the encouragement and inspiration for this book.

Racquetball

John W. Reznik

Sterling Publishing Co., Inc. · New York

Oak Tree Press Co., Ltd.
London & Sydney

GV1017. R3 R49

Other Books of Interest

Advanced Tennis
Fine Points of Tennis
Getting Started in Tennis

Handball Basics
Junior Tennis

Acknowledgments

The author wishes to thank Constantine Papadakis and George Panagiotopoulos, owners of the Imperial Court Club, Ann Arbor, Michigan, for the use of their facilities; and Craig Finger, former International Racquetball Champion, and Harold "Woody" Neighbors, resident pro, for demonstrating several of the racquetball techniques illustrated in this text. Appreciation is extended to my wife Sue and my children Kathy and Bobby who also assisted with some of the demonstrations.

Photographs by the author. Illustrations 16, 17, 18, 19, 20, 21, 24 and 130 by Bob Kalmbach.

Copyright © 1979 by Sterling Publishing Co., Inc.
Two Park Avenue, New York, N.Y. 10016
Manufactured in the United States of America
All rights reserved
Library of Congress Catalog Card No.: 78-66320
Sterling ISBN 0-8069-4138-3 Trade
4139-1 Library

Contents

9 5 0 6 9 4
EDUCATION

Illus. I. A family playing doubles.

1. The Game of Racquetball

Racquetball is a game that can be played both indoors or outdoors on a one-, three-, or four-walled court. It may be played by two players (singles), three players (cutthroat) or four players (doubles). One of the more popular and complex versions of the game is played on a four-walled, artificially lighted, rectangular indoor court.

Object of the Game

The main objective of racquetball is to hit the ball with a short-handled racquet to the front wall in such a way that your opponent will not be able to return it. You can use any of the various racquetball shots ranging from the spectacular *kill shot* to the high-percentage *pass shot*. The only restriction on the flight of the ball is that after it is hit, it must go to the front wall either directly or via the back wall, ceiling, or any side wall, but not the floor.

7

Origin of the Game

Racquetball is a very new sport; it is one of the youngest if not the youngest of the racquet games. Although still in its infancy, racquetball has already captured the hearts of millions of participants throughout North America. Today, national championships are held for men and women in both the United States and Canada.

The game was originated in the late 1940s by Joe Sobrek, a squash and tennis professional from Connecticut. He got the idea for racquetball from watching people play paddleball and thought it would be more interesting and fun to play with a strung racquet as opposed to a wooden paddle. With this in mind, Sobrek designed a racquet and got a New England racquet manufacturer to produce it. He then introduced the game and started a group of men playing at the Greenwich YMCA in Connecticut. From there the game spread rapidly throughout the United States.

During the formative years of the sport, many different balls were tried in an attempt to find the one that was best suited for the game. In the same period, national championships were held at the Greenwich YMCA. They were called the "Paddle-Rackets Championships."

As the game evolved, it was known by various names. Some called it "paddle-rackets," others "paddle-tennis," and still others "paddleball." Eventually the name evolved into its present form, "racquetball." The name stressed the words racquet and ball, the equipment used to play the game. This name finally gave the fledgling sport its own identity.

In 1968, Bob Kendler brought together the many fragmented groups and organizations that had sprung up throughout the United States since the inception of the game. The first true national racquetball championship was held the following year. It also heralded a new and phenomenal era of growth for racquetball. From approximately 50,000 players in 1970, the number of participants has swelled to over 6 million today with many more new players joining the racquetball ranks daily. The increase in players has also brought about an increase in the number of court clubs constructed in colleges and universities, Y's, private racquet clubs, and city recreational facilities. Presently, court clubs are springing up all over the United States, Canada, and around the world. With the expanded interest in play (and as a spectator sport as well) racquetball seems to be destined to continue to grow in popularity for years to come.

General Rules of Play

The rules and area of play for racquetball are similar to both handball and paddleball. The game is played until a player or team scores 21 points. A match consists of winning two of three games.

To determine the start of a match in tournament play, the referee usually tosses a coin and the winner of the coin toss has the choice of serving or receiving. During informal play, the method of determining who serves first is called *lagging for the short line* or *lagging for the back line*. When lagging, each player or team has one opportunity to win the choice of serving or receiving. To lag the ball, the player first touches the back wall with his racquet, then bounces the ball on the floor and hits it toward the front wall. The player whose rebound from the front wall bounces nearest the short line wins the choice of serving or receiving.

Play is then started with a serve from any position within the service zone (see page 170). To serve, the server drops the ball, and on its first rebound from the floor, hits the ball directly to the front wall. After the ball strikes the front wall, it must hit the floor behind the short line either before or after striking one side wall. If the ball fails to hit the front wall first, the server loses the serve.

Once a legal service is completed, the ball is *in play*. It is then struck alternately by the players or teams until one of them fails to return the ball to the front wall. The ball must be hit either on the fly or after bouncing on the floor once. After the ball is hit, it must go to the front wall, but on its way, it may strike any combination of walls or ceiling (but not the floor).

If the receiver fails to return the ball in accordance with the rules, a point is awarded to the serving side. Only the server or serving side can score points. When the server fails to return the ball successfully then a loss of serve *(side out)* occurs.

The play between each point is called a *rally*. During a rally, the ball can only be touched once by a player or team. In doubles play, both partners may swing at the ball, but only one of them may hit it.

In returning the ball, the player has free right-of-way to retrieve or hit it. Interference with this player by an opponent is considered a *hinder*. When a hinder occurs, the point is either replayed (if the hinder is unintentional) or a point or side out is awarded the offended player or team (if the hinder is intentional).

During a game, each side is allotted three 30-second time outs. When injured in a contest, a player is allowed 15 minutes rest and no time out is charged. If after 15 minutes of rest, the injured player is not able to play, then the match is awarded to his opponent. There are rest periods of 5 minutes between the first and second games of a match and 10 minutes between the second and third games.

Before playing a game or match, become familiar with the rules of play. A thorough knowledge and understanding of them will make playing racquetball more enjoyable for you, your partner and your opponent. For the complete rules of racquetball, contact your local court club or write directly to either of the racquetball governing agencies (see page 15).

Illus. 2. Singles play.

SINGLES PLAY

Singles racquetball simply pits one player against another. It is the simplest form of racquetball in terms of rules, but makes the greatest physical demands on the players. One player (determined by coin toss or lagging) serves, and if he wins the rally, scores one point and the right to serve again. If he loses the rally (side out), his opponent wins the opportunity to serve, and thus the chance to score points.

In singles, a player must be able to cover the entire court—he has no partner to rely on if a ball is hit out of his reach. This demands that he have quick reflexes (to get a good "jump" on the ball), fast feet (to run the length of the court to retrieve the ball), and great stamina (to keep running throughout the match).

DOUBLES PLAY

In doubles, two teams of two players each compete against one another. One player (chosen as above) serves while his partner must stand in the service box (see page 170) until the ball crosses the short line (see page 170). The rally continues with each team striking the ball alternately (either partner may hit the ball for his team). If the serving team wins the rally, they score one point. If they lose *(handout)*, the server's partner serves and play continues until this team again loses a rally (side out). When this occurs, the receiving team comes to serve and gets the chance to score.

This form of racquetball is less physically demanding of the players since the task of covering the court is divided between two partners. But, for this very reason, it is more difficult to win a rally with one good shot. Doubles players must therefore be able to work well as a team and make greater use of planning and strategy (see page 109).

CUTTHROAT PLAY

An interesting variation of racquetball play is called *cutthroat*, a method of play involving three players. It's good to be familiar with this game because occasionally one of the playing partners of a doubles game does not show up or a third person arrives on the scene of a singles game. The cutthroat version of racquetball is a fine way to compensate for the shortage or addition of a player.

The same rules for racquetball play apply to cutthroat with the following variations. In cutthroat, the server always plays against the other two players (Illus. 3). When the server loses the serve, the players rotate in a clockwise direction—the server moves to the right court, the player previously positioned in the right court moves to the left court and the left-court player becomes the server.

In an attempt to equalize play, the server must serve the ball to the left court when the server's score is either 0 or an even number,

Illus. 3. Cutthroat play.

and to the right court if his score is an odd number. This prevents the server from constantly serving the ball to the weaker player.

Cutthroat racquetball is not only fun to play, but is also an excellent way to improve your game and physical condition. When serving, you must cover the whole court, forcing you to play harder and run more than the receivers who are covering only half a court each. There is, however, ample opportunity to rest when receiving because you have the help of another player.

Also, playing cutthroat instead of doubles lets you play and become familiar with both sides of the court. Sometimes in doubles, players tend to be relegated to either the right or left side of the court with very little switching or play on the opposite side. Cutthroat forces you to change your position frequently and allows you to become more familiar with both sides of the court. It also enables players with dissimilar skill levels to enjoy a very competitive game. Finally, when receiving, the game forces you to learn cooperation and mutual respect for other players because you must work as a team to defeat the server. If you do not cooperate and work together, you will be unable to gain the serve and not have an opportunity to score.

The game of cutthroat is a very versatile game. It not only allows you to play when the shortage or addition of players rules out singles or doubles, but also provides you with the opportunity to practice singles and doubles play while getting a good amount of exercise.

Benefits of Play

The game of racquetball has grown in popularity every year since its inception. The reasons for its appeal are many and varied. Some people play because the rules are simple and easy to understand. Others find they can easily and quickly learn the fundamental skills and actually play a game their first time on the court. Still others participate because of the many physiological, psychological, social, and recreational benefits that can be derived from playing on a regular basis. As more and more people become aware of the benefits of racquetball and more and more courts become available, the sport will continue to increase in popularity.

One of the outstanding benefits of regular play is the improvement of physical fitness. If you play on a regular basis (three times a week for approximately 60 to 90 minutes each session) you'll find that your cardio-respiratory endurance will be significantly improved. Regular play also helps to improve your strength, flexibility, and neuro-muscular coordination. Racquetball is a high energy-consuming sport, making it an efficient way of exercising. It is an excellent year-round sport for attaining and maintaining a good level of physical fitness.

Another advantage of exercising through racquetball is the ease by which you can control the intensity of exercise. You can first decide whether you wish to play singles, cutthroat, or doubles. Singles provides the opportunity for the most vigorous workout while doubles affords the least. Cutthroat, in which you alternate between singles and doubles play, falls somewhere between the two. Whichever you choose, you can vary the intensity of play even during the match. Very few sports allow a participant to control the intensity of play so easily.

Racquetball is also an excellent means of releasing tensions and providing mental diversion. Through vigorous play, you can safely release the emotional stresses and tensions that have built up. You can relax, get away, and for a time forget the psychological pressures and tensions brought about by your job or other outside influences.

These mental benefits stem from the intense concentration that is needed to implement complex strategies of play, as well as the basics of watching and hitting the ball. Throughout the entire contest you must concentrate solely on the game in order to be successful. Trying to find an opponent's weakness and devising a method of attack in a short period of time demands undivided attention. Unlike some sports, there are no actionless periods in racquetball—there is no time to reflect upon anything other than the game. Mental satisfaction also comes from hitting a good shot, making your opponent run to retrieve the ball, maneuvering your opponent into a bad or vulnerable position on the court, or from not allowing your opponent to return the ball. It is an exhilarating feeling at the end of a match to know that you've exercised hard and played your best.

There are also some social benefits that you can derive from racquetball, such as opportunities to meet and interact with many new people. This will widen your circle of friends and increase your understanding about people in general. In racquetball, there are no ethnic restrictions or barriers imposed on a player. A male can play a female, a clerk an executive, or an employee a boss. Racquetball players are only judged by their skill, competitiveness and sportsmanship. Size and strength of an individual are also not significant factors in racquetball. The most important factor is the mastery and execution of the shots. In racquetball, a smaller player can play against a taller and bigger player and be successful.

Risk of injury is slight. Except for minor aches associated with vigorous and strenuous exercise, rarely does a player incur a major injury. This is even minimized to a greater degree when good safety practices are followed.

Racquetball is an intellectual game. It requires split-second decisions because of the speed and the different directions in which the ball travels. The ability to make sound decisions in a short period of time is a technique that can be learned and applied to everyday situations when a decision must be made in a hurry.

The equipment needed to play the game is minimal and inexpensive. All you need is a racquet, a ball, and athletic shoes. No special uniform is required.

Playing the game is just plain fun. You can play it if you are young, old, male or female. Regardless of your skill, you can still achieve success and satisfaction and have a good time doing it.

The skills needed to play the game have carry-over benefits. They can be utilized in playing sports such as paddleball, squash, badminton, tennis, and handball. These and other sports use techniques similar to those found in racquetball.

All of these values and benefits, combined with the short period of time it takes to learn to play racquetball and acquire a degree of skill, make this one of the most enjoyable sports to play.

The Racquetball Governing Agencies

There are two organizations that publish rules and govern racquetball play. They are the IRA, or International Racquetball Association, and the USRA, or United States Racquetball Association. Although their names are similar, they are rival organizations.

The IRA was formed in 1968 under the guidance and direction of Bob Kendler, a businessman from Chicago, Illinois. Through his leadership and influence, the rules and equipment for play were standardized. Kendler was also instrumental in publicizing the game through the publication of a bimonthly magazine called *Racquetball*. The first executive secretary of this association was Charles Leve who has also made numerous contributions to the development of the game.

In the early 1970s some dissent surfaced as to the management and direction of the association concerning its role and responsibilities toward the participants and future direction of the sport. As a result of this, there was a division and a new association, the USRA, was formed in 1973.

Despite their differences, both organizations sanction tournaments and are interested in the promotion and development of racquetball. Each of the associations sponsors national tournaments for men and women. They also publish magazines for racquetball enthusiasts. *National Racquetball* is the title of the publication put out by the USRA, while the IRA still publishes *Racquetball*.

While the IRA sponsors amateur competition, the USRA is concerned with both amateur and professional play. To assist them with governing professional play, the USRA has established another sanctioning body under their jurisdiction called the NRC, or National Racquetball Club. This organization is primarily responsible for governing the professional racquetball tour.

For more information about either association, contact any racquetball court club. They should be able to provide you with information about each association and membership fees. Or you can write directly to either of these agencies at the following addresses:

International Racquetball Association
2670 Union, Suite 728
Memphis, Tennessee 38112

United States Racquetball Association
4101 Dempster Street
Skokie, Illinois 60076

2. The Court

Illus. 4.
Photo courtesy of COURTIME, Lyndhurst, New Jersey.

The opportunities to play are increasing each year. More and more courts are being constructed and are available on a year-round basis. Courts are located in community recreation centers, private court clubs, health spas, Y's, military bases, high schools, and colleges and universities.

The Four-Wall Court

A standard or regulation four-wall court is an enclosed room, artificially lighted and exactly the same as a four-wall handball court both in construction and design. Various materials are employed in court construction. Concrete, fiberglass, wood, hard plaster, shatterproof glass or a combination of these materials are commonly used. The majority of courts have hardwood floors, but more recently synthetic surfaces have been introduced. Side walls are usually constructed from the traditional materials mentioned above or from glass. The use of the glass walls in court construction has facilitated instruction and increased the popularity of the game by providing many more people the opportunity to see the games.

The regulation four-wall court (Illus. 5) is retangular in shape, measuring 40 feet in length and 20 feet in width. The front and side

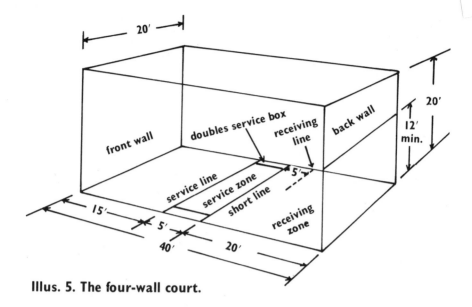

Illus. 5. The four-wall court.

walls are 20 feet high and the back wall must be at least 12 feet high.

Every player should be familiar with the markings on the court before starting to play. In the middle of the court, 20 feet from both the front and back walls is the *short line*. This line extends the width of the court and divides it into two equal parts. Five feet in front of and parallel to the short line is another line extending the width of the floor known as the *service line*. The area of the court between the outer edges of the short and service lines is called the *service zone*.

In the service zone are two boxes. These boxes, 18 inches wide and 5 feet long, are situated on each side of the service zone. They are called *service boxes* and are only used during doubles play. The server's partner must stand in one of the service boxes until the ball is served.

There are 2- to 3-inch vertical markings at the base of each side wall, 5 feet behind the short line. An imaginary line extends the width of the floor connecting these two markings and is called the *receiving line*. The area between the receiving line and the back wall is the *receiving zone*. This is the area where the player receiving the serve must stand until the ball is served.

The One-Wall Court

Although racquetball is primarily played on a four-wall court, it can also be played on a court having only one wall. The one-wall racquetball court is smaller than a four-wall court—34 feet long and 20 feet wide. The front wall measures 16 feet high and 20 feet wide with a 4-foot wire fence running along the top to help stop shots that are hit too high (Illus. 6).

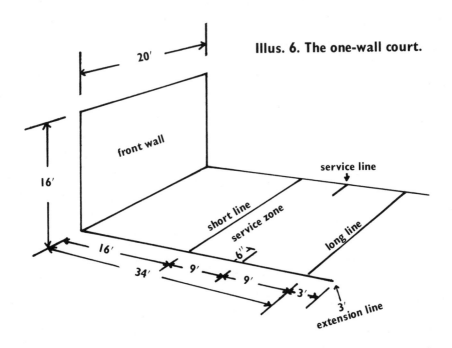

Illus. 6. The one-wall court.

The few markings on the court deal mainly with the serve. The short line is 16 feet from the front wall and is parallel to it. The service line is marked by two 6-inch lines 9 feet behind the short line, and the service zone is, as on the four-wall court, between the service and short lines. Note that on the one-wall court, the service zone extends behind the short line, while on the four-wall court it is in front of the short line.

The boundary lines on each side of the court are called the *sidelines* while the line that marks the end of the court is called the *end* or *long line*. The area between the service and end lines is the receiving zone. The receiver or receiving team must stand in this area until the ball is served.

One-wall courts are generally located outdoors and constructed of concrete, although other materials can be used. When found indoors, any of the combination of materials used in the construction of four-wall courts can be used.

The Three-Wall Court

The regulation three-wall court is similar to the one-wall court in construction and design—the length and width of the court and front wall are exactly the same. But in addition, side walls are added to the court.

There are two types of side walls that are found on three-wall courts. The first type is a partial wall which does not extend the length of the court. This wall is designed to slant downward from the front wall to a height of six feet at the short line where the wall stops (Illus. 7).

The second type of three-wall court has side walls that are equal in height to the front wall and extend the full length of the court.

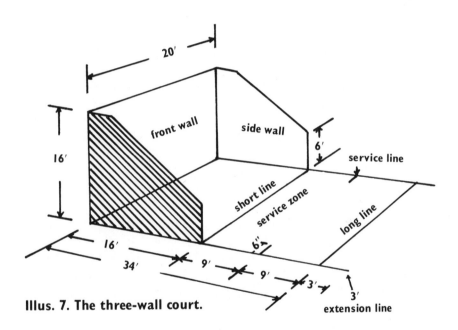

Illus. 7. The three-wall court.

3. Equipment

Illus. 8. Equipment bag.

To enhance your enjoyment, always use the proper equipment—it may even improve your caliber of play. Racquetball equipment comes in various prices and degrees of quality and is readily available at sporting goods stores, discount stores and court clubs. In order to purchase equipment to meet your needs, you should understand some of the criteria of selecting quality equipment to help you to make a better choice and, when possible, enlist the help of a racquetball professional, or at least an experienced player.

Clothing

When compared to other sports, the clothing needed for racquetball is relatively simple and inexpensive. Men usually wear shorts and a short-sleeved shirt, while women wear either a blouse with a skirt or shorts or a short dress similar to a tennis dress. For tournament play, the color of clothing worn, as dictated by the official rules of play, may be either white or light-colored. During informal play, it is also best to wear light-colored clothing so the ball can be easily seen and not lost in the background of a dark-colored uniform.

When choosing appropriate clothing to play racquetball, select clothes that fit loosely, but are not baggy. Tight-fitting clothes will hamper your performance, inhibit body movement and may cause embarrassment on the court should they rip during a sudden bending or turning movement. The material of the clothing should be highly absorbent to soak up perspiration. If excessive perspiration is not absorbed by the clothes, it will fall to the floor and perhaps cause the players to slip on the wet floor and injure themselves.

Illus. 9. Choose appropriate clothing to play racquetball.

In addition, you can wear head and wrist bands made of an absorbent material. Head bands keep both hair and sweat out of your eyes and off eyeglasses and wrist bands prevent perspiration from running down your arm and making the palm of your hand slippery and the racquet difficult to hold. Sometimes a leather glove, often with the fingers cut off, is useful to aid in gripping the racquet.

On cold days or just for warming up, some players wear sweat suits or warm-up suits to produce a light sweat and prime the body for play. Before starting actual play, the warm-up or sweat suit should be removed since it is too cumbersome and restricts body movement.

Illus. 10. Sweat suits can be worn on cold days or just for warming up.

21

Socks and Shoes

Racquetball is a game that requires many sudden starts, stops and frequent changes in direction. These quick movements cause friction between the feet, socks, and shoes which in turn can lead to painful blisters and sore feet. To help prevent this, wear medium or heavyweight wool or synthetic-blend socks and properly fitting shoes. The socks should be clean and dry to prevent infections such as athlete's foot and highly absorbent to soak up perspiration. For sensitive or tender feet, two pairs of socks can be worn to cushion the feet and provide added comfort.

In addition to the socks, properly fitting shoes not only help to prevent blisters, but also give your ankles ample support and provide good traction which is so necessary to prevent slipping. Shoes worn for play may be either low-cut or high-topped. The majority of players prefer the low-cut version because they are lighter, but players with a history of weak ankles should wear the high-topped shoes because of the added support they give the ankles. The bottom of the shoes should have rippled, as opposed to smooth, rubber soles. The rippled sole provides greater shock-absorbency and increased traction for easier maneuverability on the court. Shoes should not have black soles because they will mark and scuff the floors.

At the conclusion of play, air out your shoes so they will dry before the next contest. This will not only lengthen the life of the shoes, but also helps to prevent the growth of fungi and makes them more comfortable to wear.

The Racquet

Selecting the proper racquet is of prime importance for racquetball players—choosing the wrong racquet can significantly affect your performance. The racquet is the link between you and the ball; hence, if you do not have a strong link, your performance will suffer. You are only as good as your weakest link.

When choosing a racquet, buy one of good quality. There are several companies that manufacture a wide variety of high-quality racquets, and prices vary, with the better racquets generally costing more. The novice player can either buy an inexpensive racquet or, better yet, rent better quality racquets at a racquetball club, sampling many different models. The trouble with purchasing an inexpensive racquet is its lack of durability. It may also not play as well as a better racquet, resulting in discouragement and frustration.

Illus. II. When choosing a racquet, buy one of good quality that feels comfortable in your hand.

Selecting a suitable racquet can be rather confusing. Before purchasing any racquet, consult a racquetball professional. He can make you aware of the various factors to be considered when selecting a racquet that will meet your specific needs.

Although all racquets must meet the specifications as stipulated by the rules, they can be constructed from different materials and come in various shapes and weights. There are racquets with oval-, round-, rectangular-, and teardrop-shaped heads. They are made of wood, metal, fiberglass, graphite, or a combination of these materials. Some racquets are stiff, some whippy, some heavy and some light. Racquet grips also vary and range in size from 3-15/16 inches to 4-5/8 inches in circumference. The grips are usually covered in leather or rubber and some have perforations while others have indentations or ridges to make it easier to hold the racquet when your hand is perspiring.

In addition, you should also understand the characteristics of the racquet in relation to the type of game you want to, and are able to, play. For example, stiff or rigid racquets generally give you better control while whippy or flexible racquets give added power. Racquets that are heavy and long also add power while light and smaller ones allow you to swing faster during rallies.

When purchasing a racquet, select one that you can handle easily. Racquets usually weigh between 8 and 12 ounces. You should gen-

Illus. 12. The correct grip size.

Illus. 13. The grip is too small.

Illus. 14. The grip is too large.

erally begin with a light racquet. The heavier the racquet, the stronger you will have to be to use it. A racquet that is too heavy will cause undue strain on your arm and elbow, resulting in improper stroking and possible injury. If your arm hurts after playing, your racquet might be too heavy. On the other hand, the racquet should not be so light that it causes you to overswing or overhit the ball.

The grip should feel comfortable in your hand. It should be small enough to allow you to snap your wrist easily, but if it is too small, it will have a tendency to twist in your hand. To check for the proper grip size, hold the racquet with a forehand grip (see page 28) as if you were shaking hands with it. If your thumb is wrapped around the racquet and it rests on the first section of your middle finger, you have the correct grip (see Illus. 12). The grip is too small if the thumb passes the first knuckle of the middle finger (see Illus. 13), and too large if it does not touch it or barely touches it (see Illus. 14).

The type of material selected for the grip handle is a matter of personal preference. Many players prefer the leather grip because it conforms better to the hand. The rubber grip, however, may be more desirable if you perspire a lot.

The string used in racquets is made of nylon; it is very durable and maintains a fairly stable tension. The tension used to string a racquet ranges from 18 to 35 pounds. The amount or degree of string tension needed is determined by a player's skill level and personal preference. It should be pointed out that a higher string tension adds more power to your shots but it is also more difficult to control. In racquetball, gut strings are not used. They are expensive and do not have any advantage over nylon strings.

When buying a racquet, it may be wise to purchase a metal one as it is more durable than the other types. Metal racquets last longer because they can absorb more punishment and abuse caused by contacts with the walls and will only bend in situations where racquets made of other materials will break.

The Ball

The official ball used in tournament play is 2¼ inches in diameter, weighs approximately 1.40 ounces and bounces 68 to 72 inches high when dropped from a height of 100 inches at a temperature of 76° F by USRA standards or 70 to 74° F by IRA standards. It is made from rubber molded into two cups and sealed together at the edges. The inside of the ball is hollow and inflated with compressed air or gas.

A black ball is used in nearly all sanctioned tournaments while professional tournaments use a green one. For tournament play, the ball must be approved by the racquetball governing agency sanctioning the tournament. During informal play, either the black or green ball is suitable. Recently blue and red balls have been introduced and are primarily used during informal play. With the approval of the presiding racquetball governing body, they can also be utilized in tournament competition.

Prior to play, each ball should be examined to make sure that it meets the specifications as stated in the rules. When a ball does not have similar characteristics or rebound qualities as those described in the rules, it should not be used in tournament play because it can significantly alter the complexion of play and influence the outcome of the game or match. Balls that are not perfectly round or that are dead or excessively lively will tend to bounce erratically and influence play.

Before a match begins, the referee chooses the ball for play after checking them carefully. Two or more additional balls should be selected as a precautionary measure so that in case a ball breaks or leaves the court during play, the match can continue without a prolonged interruption. During the course of a game, at the request of the players or teams and at the discretion of the referee, a change of balls may take place.

Safety Equipment

Racquetball is a relatively safe sport to play. To make it even safer, be sure to use the proper safety equipment described below.

Safety thong: This is the loop located at the end of the racquet handle. Wear it securely around your wrist during play to prevent the racquet from flying from your hand and possibly striking your opponent.

Eye guards: Getting hit with the racquet or with the ball traveling at a high rate of speed can be very dangerous. Eye guards should be worn to prevent the ball or racquet from contacting the eye. Usually, eye guards are made of plastic or thick metal wire. They are lightweight and do not obstruct vision. It is highly recommended that you wear them, especially if you are a beginner or wear glasses or contact lenses. Several different styles are available.

Eye glasses: If you wear glasses while playing, always take precautionary measures to protect your eyes. Wear glasses that have shatter-proof lenses and always use eye guards. Although the eye guard may seem inconvenient, it is vital to prevent injury. Also secure your glasses firmly with an elastic retaining device or a similar method to prevent them from slipping and falling to the floor.

Gloves: A glove worn on the racquet hand during play can help to absorb perspiration and prevent the racquet handle from becoming slippery and hard to hold. During hot weather and vigorous play, a glove may become so soaked that you will be unable to hold the racquet. If this occurs, change gloves immediately.

Illus. 15. Be sure to use proper safety equipment.

Dry rosin: This substance can be applied to a racquet handle to help keep it from slipping from your hand.

Wrist bands: Wearing a wrist band is another method that helps keep perspiration off the hand. The band absorbs perspiration running down the arm and prevents it from reaching the hand.

Head bands: Head bands are worn for two reasons—they prevent sweat from going into your eyes and blurring your vision, and they keep your hair out of your eyes so you can see the ball better.

Before playing a game, check to see that you have the proper safety equipment. It will make your game more enjoyable when you know that you have minimized the risk of injury.

4. Hitting the Ball

The racquetball stroke is not a single technique, but a set of coordinated techniques. You must be able to grip the racquet properly, step into position quickly, and execute the appropriate stroke correctly. It is only after you master these fundamentals that you will be able to hit the ball with accuracy and consistency.

The Grips

The grip is the basic foundation upon which an efficient stroke is built—poor technique in gripping the racquet leads to inconsistent strokes. When analyzing a player's stroke to determine why errors occur, the grip is often overlooked. It is, however, a vital component of the stroke and should not be neglected.

Mastering the proper grip is important because it is the connection between you and the racquet. This connection influences every shot you make; it is the link that allows for a smooth transfer of power from the body to the racquet.

Although you may be successful with almost any grip at times, the best grip is the one which produces the greatest number of good strokes and the fewest failures. Experience has shown that certain methods of gripping the racquet are better than others because they produce the highest percentage of successful shots. Pay careful attention to learning the correct grips for the forehand and backhand strokes before attempting any shots. If you develop bad habits from the start, they will be difficult to overcome later.

THE FOREHAND GRIP

The method used to hold the racquet for forehand shots is referred to as the "shake-hands" grip. This grip is similar to the forehand grip in other racquet sports such as badminton, tennis and squash. The shake-hands grip is very functional—it permits easy movement of the wrist and gives the fingers good control over the racquet.

To assume the forehand grip, place the racquet on edge so the short strings of the racquet are perpendicular to the floor. Then grasp the handle with the playing hand as if you were shaking hands with it. The palm of the hand should lie behind the large flat plane of the handle. When you hold the racquet properly, the handle runs diagonally across your palm with the butt of the racquet at the heel of your hand and the upper portion of the handle resting on your fingers.

Wrap your thumb and fingers around the handle spreading your fingers comfortably apart with your index finger slightly farther away from the other three fingers as if it were a trigger finger. Wrap your thumb around the handle diagonally across the back side of it so that it rests between the first and second fingers. At the top of the racquet handle, a "V" is formed by the index finger and thumb. Throughout the entire stroke, hold the racquet firmly, especially at the moment of impact, to prevent the racquet from twisting and turning in your hand. The proper grip will not only allow you to hit the ball squarely, but will also give you added power and more control (Illus. 16-18).

Illus. 16.

Illus. 17.

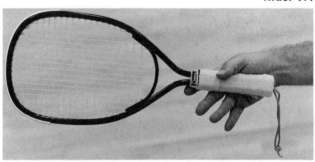

The forehand grip.

Illus. 18.

Illus. 20.

The backhand grip.

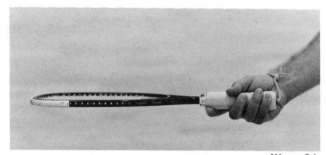

Illus. 19.

Illus. 21.

THE BACKHAND GRIP

For backhand shots, most racquetball players adjust their grips slightly. If you don't change your grip, you will have to make an adjustment in your swing or your ball will tend to angle upward. The resulting loss of power and accuracy, along with the angle of the ball, will probably set your opponent up for an easy return. To hit a backhand with a forehand grip requires a flatter swing. It also requires you to contact the ball earlier in the swing (closer to the back hip). Combined, these factors give you less margin for error in the swing, with a small error in timing resulting in a badly misplayed shot.

The grip that is recommended and commonly used for backhand shots is called the "palms-down" grip. From the forehand grip, turn your hand counterclockwise (clockwise if you are left-handed) about a quarter of a turn until the "V" formed by your index finger and thumb is on the inner edge of the racquet. The fingers should be spread comfortably and wrapped around the racquet handle with the index finger slightly away from the other fingers and the thumb lying diagonally across the back side of the handle and resting on the middle finger. The large knuckle of the index finger should rest on the outer bevel of the racquet handle when the racquet face is perpendicular to the ground (Illus. 19-21).

Although this grip may feel uncomfortable at first, it will allow you to hit the ball squarely and make your shots more efficiently. The racquet should also be held firmly throughout the entire stroke, especially when contacting the ball. Otherwise it might turn in your hand causing you to lose control of your shots.

THE ONE-GRIP SYSTEM

Many racquetball players utilize a "one-grip" system of holding the racquet for both forehand and backhand strokes. That is, they do not change their grip, but hold the racquet with the same grip for every shot they take. Some of these players use either the standard forehand (or shake-hands) grip, while others use the conventional palms-down (backhand) grip. Still others use a compromise grip, somewhere between the usual forehand and backhand grips.

Players who use the one-grip approach feel that it eliminates some of the problems associated with changing grips, believing that there is not enough time to change grips during the course of a rally. However, with practice, most players can change grips quite easily and quickly.

The Ready Position

The ready position in racquetball is the stance that a player assumes while waiting to return a serve or a shot during play. It allows complete freedom for instantaneous movement and quick maneuverability on the court. From the ready position, a player can move swiftly in any direction—front, back, sideways—to retrieve or return the ball during the course of a rally with either a forehand or backhand stroke.

To get ready to receive, stand alertly in a position facing the front wall. Spread your feet comfortably apart, parallel to each other with your weight evenly distributed over them. The equal distribution of weight contributes to good balance and provides freedom of movement.

When positioning your feet, start with them shoulder-width apart and adjust the stance from there. Many players find shoulder width a comfortable position, others like their feet spread a little wider, while some like them closer together. The foot position you assume will be dictated by your body build. Adjust your foot position until you find the one that is comfortable for you. Set them far enough apart to keep you well-balanced, but not so far that your movement from the ready stance is restricted.

Next bend your knees and hips slightly. This flexed body position will enable you to move after the ball instantaneously. This is important because the knees must first be flexed before you can step and the flexed hip position helps you to stay relaxed and keep your body low when moving to hit the ball. A common error made by racquetball players is to stand upright with legs straight and knees locked. This causes them to lose precious time that is often needed to get into position to hit. By keeping the body flexed you can save time in moving after the ball—any time that can be saved might mean the difference between returning the ball and missing it.

Hold the racquet with either a forehand or backhand grip in front of you. You can hold the throat of the racquet with the non-racquet hand if you like. Bend your arms at the elbows for the same reason that you flex your knees and hips. A flexed elbow will save you time when moving your arm backwards in preparation for the forward

Illus. 22. The ready position.

swing, since in order to hit the ball you must first bend your elbow. If you start with your elbow straight, you will have to use two movements to get your racquet into position to hit the ball.

Now make sure you are standing in a relaxed manner. If the stance is too rigid, it will cause you to expend more energy and thus you will tire more quickly.

Your eyes should be focused on the ball; keep watching it until the rally is over. By watching the ball, you will be able to anticipate its flight and move into the proper hitting position to return it with authority.

All racquetball players assume a ready position when waiting to return the ball. However, they adjust and vary their stance to fit their own body build and style of play. You should experiment to find out which ready position is comfortable and best suited for your needs.

POINTS TO REMEMBER

• Stand facing the front wall.

• Spread feet comfortably apart.

• Keep feet parallel to each other.

• Flex knees and hips.

• Distribute body weight evenly.

• Hold racquet waist-high in front of you.

• Keep body relaxed, not rigid.

• Focus eyes on the ball.

Wrist Cock

Unlike tennis, in racquetball the wrist is snapped as you contact the ball during a stroke. This is a crucial factor in producing powerful and accurate shots. You must snap your wrist forcefully in order to generate speed on the ball. This extra movement added to the already powerful arm swing gives added momentum to the ball. The wrist motion is similar to the wrist action used in throwing a baseball.

To prepare the wrist during the stroke, cock it as you bring your

Illus. 23. The wrist cock on the forehand side.

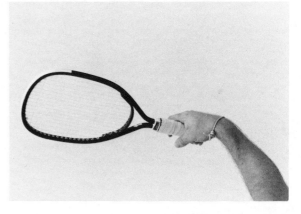

Illus. 24. The wrist cock on the backhand side.

racquet behind your body for the backswing. The wrist is cocked on the forehand side by extending it (bending it back), while on the backhand side it is cocked by flexing it (bending it inwards) (see Illus. 23 and 24). Although you may have some success hitting the ball with a fixed wrist, you will not generate much power and the lack of speed on the ball will make your shots easier for your opponent to retrieve and return. During a fast rally, you may not have time to fully cock your wrist. When this occurs, hit with a firm wrist and rotate it forward through the ball as contact is made. But whenever possible, the wrist should be fully cocked and snapped during the stroke.

The Strokes

There are four basic strokes that you need to learn and master in order to execute the different shots and serves that are used during play. These are the forehand, the backhand, the overhand, and the underhand. It is important to understand the fundamentals of executing each stroke and to know when to use them during a match. These strokes are the building blocks upon which a sound racquetball game is built.

The stroke that you use at any given time depends upon several factors—the height and speed of the ball, your court position, your opponent's position, the type of shot to be hit, and so on. Generally, all shots below shoulder level are hit with either a forehand or backhand sidearm stroke, balls that drop below knee level are hit with either a sidearm or underhand stroke and balls above shoulder height are hit with an overhand stroke.

THE FOREHAND STROKE

The forehand is probably the single most important stroke in racquetball. This stroke is relied upon and used more often and under a greater number of circumstances than any other stroke; it is used both for serving and during a rally. Many racquetball players, even professionals, prefer to use the forehand whenever possible. Players have even been known (and often prefer) to run around their backhands when they have time to hit a forehand, even when the ball is just 2 or 3 feet from the side wall.

For a good forehand stroke, it is important to grip the racquet correctly. Use the forehand or shake-hands grip previously described. This has proven to be the most successful grip for hitting forehand shots.

After gripping the racquet correctly, move from the ready position (see page 31) to the proper hitting stance facing the side wall. As you pivot, shift your body weight to the back foot, swing the racquet arm back to a position approximately waist-high or higher behind your body and rotate the hips and shoulders slightly towards the back wall. The hip and shoulder rotation serves as a wind-up and helps both to initiate a smooth swing and add power to the stroke. Remember to cock your wrist during the backswing. At this point, the racquet head should be tilted upwards, the elbow flexed and the wrist cocked. The feet should be spread comfortably apart and the knees and hips flexed (Illus. 25).

The forward movement of the swing begins by pushing off the rear leg and stepping toward the oncoming ball. As you step forward, transfer your body weight to the front foot, rotate your shoulders and hips and swing the racquet forward to meet the ball (Illus. 26). This

35

Illus. 25 and 26. Spread your feet . . . step forward onto your front foot.

movement will bring the racquet into the hitting area. During the forward swing, gradually lower your body and racquet to the height of the oncoming ball by bending at the knees. As the racquet arm moves forward to meet the ball, the wrist should still be cocked and the elbow of the arm leads the swing followed by the wrist and then the racquet. During the swing, the arm should be kept parallel to the floor while holding the racquet face flat (Illus. 27).

In this, as in all of the other strokes, begin to snap your wrist just before the racquet contacts the ball. Snap your wrist forcefully and fully extend your arm. The ball should be contacted at a point directly opposite or slightly in front of the forward hip. Keep the non-racquet arm to the side of your body and away from the racquet—this permits you to swing the racquet freely (Illus. 28).

After you hit the ball, the arm swing continues in the direction the ball is hit, then slightly around and away from the body. Transfer your body weight completely to the forward foot while the rear leg lags behind for balance (Illus. 29). Throughout the entire follow-through, stay low and continue your swing as if hitting through the ball (Illus. 30). This will better enable you to control the speed, height and direction of the ball. The follow-through is very important because it adds continuity to the shot. An abrupt follow-through or no follow-through will cause your shots to go astray. During the entire swing, especially when hitting the ball, be sure to hold the racquet with a firm grip. This will prevent the racquet from turning or slipping from your hand.

Illus. 27 and 28. Swing holding the racquet face flat and . . .

Illus. 29 and 30. . . . transfer your weight to the forward foot. Continue your swing as if hitting through the ball.

37

THE BACKHAND STROKE

Developing a good backhand stroke is essential for success in racquetball. If you don't master backhand, you will be at the mercy of your opponent, since most players try to concentrate on serving and rallying to their opponent's weak side and in most instances, this is the backhand side. To compensate for a weak backhand, players attempt to "run around" it and hit the return with a forehand stroke. This is not always feasible because the side wall may be too close, or you may be forced out of position. The extra running will also cause you to tire more quickly. Then too, the ball is often returned so fast you do not have enough time to run around the shot.

A good backhand stroke begins by using the proper grip. The recommended grip is the backhand or palms-down grip described earlier in this chapter. The one-grip method can also be used by players with strong hands and wrists or in instances when there is not enough time to change from a forehand to a backhand grip.

To hit a backhand shot, pivot from the ready position (page 31) to a hitting stance facing the side wall. Swing the forward leg across the body so that the feet line up in the direction of the oncoming ball. This position is similar to batting the ball left-handed in baseball. During the pivot, bring your racquet arm back about waist-high behind your body, flex your elbow, cock your wrist and keep the head of the racquet tilted upward, pointing toward the back wall. Rotate your shoulders and hips and shift your body weight to the rear foot. Keep the knees and hips flexed and the feet comfortably spread apart (Illus. 31).

This hitting stance allows you a free and unrestricted swing toward the ball and lets you uncoil rapidly to add more power to your shot. How far you rotate your hips and the amount of backswing you can take will depend on how much time you have to set up for the shot.

Start the forward swing by pushing off the back foot and stepping in the direction of the ball with the forward foot (Illus. 32). At the same time, start shifting your body weight forward to the front leg. Begin the hip and shoulder rotation, closely followed by the forward movement of the racquet arm. Swing the racquet arm smoothly and forcefully, with the racquet moving out and away from the body to contact the ball. During the forward swing, the elbow leads the arm, followed by the wrist and then the racquet (Illus. 33). During the swing, the racquet head is kept parallel to the floor.

Begin the wrist snap as you approach contact and at the moment of impact, the arm should be fully extended and the wrist

Illus. 31.

Illus. 32.

Illus. 33.

Keep the knees and hips flexed . . .
step in the direction of the ball with
the forward foot . . . begin the hip and
shoulder rotation.

Illus. 34

Illus. 35.

Illus. 36.

On impact the arm should be fully extended . . . contact the ball opposite or forward of the front hip . . . swing the racquet around and to the side of your body.

snapped (Illus. 34). Contact the ball either opposite or slightly forward of the front hip (Illus. 35). As with the forehand, the racquet should be held firmly to prevent it from twisting or slipping from your hand.

As the ball rebounds from your racquet, continue to follow through—do not stop your swing abruptly. Continue the swing as long as possible in the intended direction of the shot. This will allow for a smooth swing and better control of the shot. The racquet then continues around and to the side of your body (Illus. 36). Although the follow-through should be as long as possible, it should not be exaggerated. A wide, sweeping follow-through can create a dangerous situation for your opponent and should be avoided if possible.

Mastering the backhand stroke is essential for the development of a well-rounded game. Practice it diligently until it becomes a powerful offensive weapon and not merely a defensive shot to keep the ball in play. A good backhand stroke will allow you to return many more shots by saving you time and steps in getting to the ball.

THE UNDERHAND STROKE

Hitting balls that drop below knee level is best accomplished by use of the underhand stroke, a stroke which allows a player to impart a great deal of power on the ball. It can be performed on either the forehand or backhand side.

The primary function of the underhand stroke is offensive. It is used interchangeably with the sidearm swing to hit kill shots when the ball is knee-high or lower. Sometimes it is employed as a defensive weapon to return low shots to the ceiling. Other shots that can be hit with this stroke are the lob and lob serve. The same fundamentals used for the other strokes apply to hitting the underhand.

After gripping the racquet correctly, pivot from the ready position to a hitting stance facing the side wall. As you pivot, transfer your body weight to the rear foot and move the racquet arm back to a position behind the body about waist-high or higher. In this stance, the knees and hips are slightly flexed and the feet are spread comfortably apart. This will insure the low body position so necessary for hitting low shots. Keep the elbow of the racquet arm bent slightly, the wrist cocked and the head of the racquet pointing upward. The hips and shoulders are rotated a little to help impart greater force on the ball (Illus. 37).

The forward swing is started by pushing off the back leg and stepping toward the ball (Illus. 38). At the same time, the racquet swings forward and down as the hips and shoulders turn to bring the racquet into position to hit the ball (Illus. 39).

At the moment of contact, snap your wrist and fully extend your arm. Hold the racquet firmly to prevent it from either slipping or twisting in the hand. As the ball is contacted, the racquet head points toward the floor (Illus. 40). Continue the swing as long and low as possible toward the front wall in the direction the ball is hit (Illus. 41). This will help increase the accuracy and low placement of the shot. Follow through completely—forward and up and across the body toward the opposite shoulder. At the end of the follow-through, the body weight is completely shifted to the front foot while the back leg stays behind to maintain balance (Illus. 42).

THE OVERHAND STROKE

The overhand stroke is generally hit on the forehand side to hit balls at shoulder level or above. This stroke is primarily used to return shots to the ceiling, but occasionally, it is used for hitting pass shots. Rarely is it useful for hitting kill shots.

Illus. 37. Keep the elbows of the racquet arm bent slightly.

Illus. 38.

Illus. 39.

Illus. 40.

Step towards the ball . . .
swing the racquet forward
. . . as you contact the ball,
the racquet head should
point towards the floor.

43

Illus. 4I and 42. Continue the swing . . . at the end of the follow-through shift the body weight to the front foot.

To execute the overhand, grasp the racquet with the proper forehand grip, then maneuver yourself into position to hit the ball by pivoting to a hitting stance facing the side wall (Illus. 43).

The toes of the pivot (rear) foot should point toward the side wall while the forward foot points in the direction of the oncoming ball. As you pivot, shift your body weight over the rear foot and bring the racquet arm back behind the body. Keep the elbow bent at a 90° angle and the wrist cocked. The other (non-hitting) arm is raised slightly forward from your body to give balance. The body position is similar to an individual throwing a ball (Illus. 44).

Start the forward swing by pushing off the rear leg and stepping toward the ball with the forward foot. Start the racquet swing upward to meet the ball—the elbow leads the motion followed by the wrist and then the racquet (Illus. 45).

Time the forward swing to contact the ball about 6 to 12 inches in front of your body. Again, just before impact, begin to snap your wrist to add more power to the shot. Extend the racquet arm fully with the grip firm and the racquet face flat (Illus. 46).

After the ball is hit, the racquet should continue to move as far as possible in the direction of the shot (Illus. 47). Then follow through down and across your body toward the knee of the forward foot (Illus. 48). It is essential to have a good follow-through, as it gives added control to the stroke.

Illus. 43 and 44. In the overhand stroke, grasp the racquet with the proper forehand grip . . . the body position is similar to a person throwing a ball.

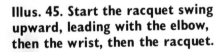

Illus. 45. Start the racquet swing upward, leading with the elbow, then the wrist, then the racquet.

Illus. 46.

Illus. 47.

Illus. 48.

Extend the racquet arm fully . . . the racquet continues to move in the direction of the shot . . . follow through down and across your body.

Footwork

One of the most neglected areas in racquetball is the understanding and implementation of proper footwork. Proper footwork will allow you to get to the ball, execute an effective shot from a balanced hitting stance and return to a good defensive court position after the shot. In short, learning and mastering proper footwork will enable you to use your body in a more effective and efficient manner on the court.

MOVING TO THE BALL

Moving into position to hit the ball is also a prime requisite for success in racquetball. A perfect stroke means nothing if you cannot get to the right place to use it. Proper footwork involves moving from the ready position quickly and easily to a position to hit the ball. There are several different types of steps that can be used for this during play. Some are more efficient than others for moving in various directions, but all methods should be mastered.

Two key factors in moving to hit the ball are proper court position and stance. Proper court position will be covered in depth in Chapter 6—*Receiving and Returning the Serve* and in Chapter 8—*Strategy.* The correct stance for waiting to move for the ball is the ready stance previously described.

The footwork involved in moving forward or backward is the easiest to learn—it is something that you do every day. You simply run or walk to the place where you intend to hit the ball. When starting to run forward after the ball, you merely push off with either foot and run in the appropriate direction as fast as you can while keeping your body under control. When you get to the spot where you want to hit the ball, plant your rear foot, step toward the ball and swing. If you do not plant the rear foot, you will not have very good control of your body or your shot. It is important that you stop, plant your foot and then step toward the oncoming ball. Otherwise, you might overrun the shot causing the ball to be too close to you and forcing you to use a cramped swing.

To move to the backcourt after the ball, simply pivot and either step or run to the position where you want to hit the ball. The procedure of stopping, planting the foot and stepping toward the ball is the same as used when running forward. In addition, you must try to step in the direction of your intended shot when moving to meet the ball.

When balls are hit near the side wall, you can either use a cross-over step or a sliding movement. The sliding method is known as "side-shuffling" and is similar to the technique used in basketball. This method is only used when a few steps are necessary to reach the ball and not to retrieve balls that are far away because the movement is slow and awkward.

To side-step, keep your feet parallel and close to the floor and take quick sliding steps. First step away with one leg and then quickly slide the other leg next to it. Continue doing this until you reach the ball. Then pivot on the foot on the same side as the ball and step toward it with the other leg. This sliding-shuffle movement can be used to move to either side or even toward the front or backcourt when retrieving the ball.

Remember, it is essential to learn to move efficiently into position to hit the ball and to return to an advantageous position after hitting it. To assist you in improving your footwork, practice the drills found in Chapter 9.

HITTING THE BALL

To stroke the ball consistently, you must learn to coordinate your feet with your upper body and arms in order to develop a smooth swing. Proper use of the feet in relation to the other parts of the body allows you to time and coordinate your shots. Good foot movement also allows you to raise and lower your body into proper position to hit the ball and to add power to your shots by both accelerating your body and shifting your weight forward to meet the ball. When the weight is not transferred or the body is not moved forward to hit the ball, a loss of power results because you are off-balance and have less force moving forward to meet the ball. Lack of proper footwork also leads to inconsistency because it forces you to hit the ball from awkward and difficult positions, thus making the return more difficult.

Good footwork in hitting the ball includes setting up to hit the ball, transferring your weight, stepping to meet the ball and following through in a balanced position. This should be learned in the early stages of racquetball development, for it will make the strokes and shots easier to perform.

5. The Serve

The serve is the shot that initiates play and is therefore the most important shot in racquetball. The main purpose of the serve is to score an ace or to at least put your opponent on the defensive. (An ace is a served ball that eludes a receiver for an outright winner.) Too often, players take the serve for granted. They merely use it as a means of putting the ball into play and not as the powerful offensive weapon it actually is.

When executed properly, the serve allows you to remain on the offensive by either scoring a point or eliciting a weak return from your opponent. In other words, a well-executed serve leaves you momentarily in command of play; it permits you to remain in the center of the court and control the play. An ineffective serve will place you in a defensive position when your opponent's return must be retrieved from deep in the court or is killed for an outright winner.

What is an effective serve? Any serve that your opponent has trouble returning. More specifically, it is any serve that is not returned or forces a return that allows the server to remain near the short line in the center-court position and to rally effectively. A serve is also effective if the return of the service gives you a set-up off the back wall (a shot that bounces lazily from the back wall to the center of the court that you can easily return for a winner). These weak returns give you the opportunity to win the rally by executing any of the basic offensive racquetball shots.

The serve is usually considered ineffective if your opponent hits the ball with a well-placed offensive shot that drives you to the rear area of the court. By neutralizing your serve and making you retreat to the backcourt, the receiver can move to and control the center-court position. The player who controls this position usually wins the rally (see Chapter 8—*Strategy*). The serve that is least effective is the one that can be hit for an outright winner. This one should be avoided at all costs.

There are four basic serves that a player should learn and master.

They are: the power or drive serve, the lob serve, the change-up or slow drive serve and the "Z" serve. All of these serves can be performed using basic strokes. The speed, height and direction of any of these serves can be varied to improve a serve's offensive potential. The effectiveness of the serve will depend on your skill and control of the basic strokes.

Beginning the Serve

All of the above serves begin by bouncing the ball and stepping forward. This can be done with either a one-step or two-step method.

THE ONE-STEP METHOD

If you use the one-step method, then start with your body weight over the rear foot. Bring the racquet arm back about waist-high or

Illus. 49. Hold the ball about knee-high.

Illus. 50 and 51. Push off the rear foot . . . the swing should be low.

higher behind your body, the head of the racquet pointing upward. Bend the elbow of the racquet arm, cock your wrist and hold the ball about knee-high in the other hand which hangs down slightly in front of your body (Illus. 49).

To begin the forward swing, drop the ball, and as it rebounds from the floor, push off the rear foot and step forward with the front one (Illus. 50). As you step, begin the forward swing of the racquet. The swing should be low and timed to contact the ball at the top of the bounce when it is momentarily still (Illus. 51). It's important to mention at this time that the ball should be dropped and not thrown to the floor. When a ball is dropped, it will rebound to approximately the same height it was dropped from. Knowing this and keeping the bounce consistent will make it easier for you to contact the ball in the same place every time you serve.

During the forward swing, shift your body weight to the front leg (Illus. 52) and rotate at the shoulders and waist (Illus. 53). This will bring the racquet into the hitting area.

51

Illus. 52. Shift your body weight to the front leg.

Illus. 53. Rotate at the shoulders and waist.

52

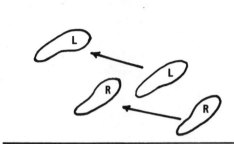

Illus. 54.

When you use the two-step method, your body weight is initially over the forward foot (Illus. 55), both arms hanging at your sides. The backswing is the same as in the one-step method, except that at the same time the racquet moves back, you step forward with the

Illus. 55. Your body weight is initially over the forward foot.

53

Illus. 56 and 57. Drop the ball from a position about knee-high . . .
push off the rear foot and step forward with the front one. Then . . .

Illus. 58.
. . . swing your racquet arm
forward.

rear foot behind your body and transfer your weight to it. Then drop the ball from a position about knee-high (Illus. 56).

As the ball bounces from the floor, push off the rear foot and step forward with the front one (Illus. 57). Swing your racquet arm forward (Illus. 58) and rotate your shoulders and hips (Illus. 59). This movement brings the racquet into position to contact the ball. Time your forward swing to contact the ball at the top of the bounce (Illus. 60)—in this position the ball is easier to hit because it is momentarily stationary.

The Power Serve

With the introduction of the "live" ball, the importance of developing a good power serve has increased significantly. Today, it has become so important and effective that it is the most widely used of all the basic serves. When hit correctly, the low trajectory, speed and

Illus. 59 and 60. Rotate your shoulders and hips . . . contact the ball at the top of the bounce, and follow through.

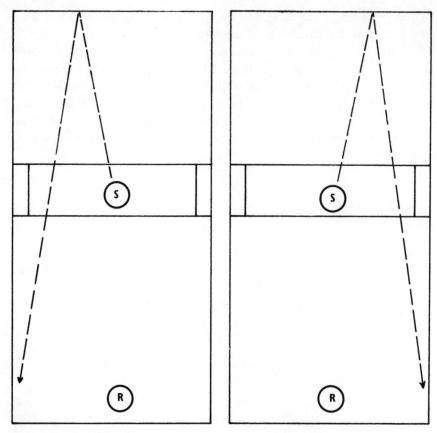

Illus. 61 and 62. The power serve rebounds off the front wall directly toward a rear corner.

direction of the ball make it one of the most, if not *the* most, difficult serves to return.

The power serve is executed by using a forceful underhand or sidearm stroke, usually from the forehand side. The ball is hit so that it rebounds low and fast from the front wall toward a rear corner of the court (Illus. 61-62).

You must hit the serve with enough power and at a low enough height for the ball to contact the floor just beyond the short line so that it takes a quick low bounce. This makes the return of serve difficult because the receiver must hurry to get to the ball before it bounces twice. On the other hand, if the ball is hit too high or bounces deep in the court, it will rebound off the back wall for an easy return.

For power serves to be effective, they must be hit low, forcefully, and angled to your opponent's weak side and away from him. Factors which can be varied to increase the effectiveness of this serve are the speed, angle, and height at which the ball is hit. By changing one, two or even all of these factors, you will help to confuse your opponent and hopefully either score an ace or force a weak return. Also, by changing the angle of the serve you can make the ball strike the side wall, creating another problem for the receiver to contend with. A well-placed ball might even strike the "crotch" or juncture where the side wall meets the floor causing the ball to rebound either in an erratic manner or very close to the floor, making the return even more difficult.

To execute a power serve, take a position in the service zone near the center of the court. This position will allow you enough room to send the serve to either side of the court without revealing your intentions to your opponent. Hold the racquet with the forehand grip and stand in a relaxed position facing the side wall.

Keep your knees and hips flexed with your feet spread comfortably apart. The shoulder of your non-racquet arm should point to the spot where the ball will contact the front wall. The low body position and the pointing of the shoulder help to insure a low and accurate hit on the front wall and a powerful stroke.

Keep your body weight primarily over the front or back foot, depending on whether you use a one-step or two-step method for the serve. In either case, snap your wrist at the moment the ball is hit to impart greater velocity on the ball. Your grip must be firm, especially at the instant of impact. This will help you to control the ball by preventing the racquet from moving or slipping in your hand.

After the ball is hit, the racquet continues forward toward the front wall. Your follow-through should be as long and as low as possible in the direction the ball is hit. This helps with the accuracy of the shot and helps to prevent you from hitting the ball upward before it leaves the racquet. The follow-through continues until the racquet comes to rest on the other side of your body.

The Angle Serve

The angle serve is a variation of the power serve and uses the same technique. Either the one- or two-step method can be used.

For an angle serve, the ball is hit so that it rebounds from the front wall to the side wall without striking the floor (Illus. 63). The serve is

57

hit low and hard so that the rebound from the side wall will be very low and fast. If you are lucky, it will hit the crack and skid near the floor, making the return almost impossible. This serve should be practiced until you can consistently hit the ball low. Eventually you will hit the crack many times during a game and it will be your skill, not luck, that causes this to happen. When used in combination with the power serve (which goes directly to the rear corner of the court) the angle serve can be very effective. An opponent who has difficulty in returning the straight power serve will move to a position near the side wall to wait to receive it. Instead of hitting another straight power serve to that side, you can either hit a straight power serve to the opposite side, or an angle serve. The angle serve will strike the side wall before it can be returned and the rebound will probably jam your opponent, preventing an effective return.

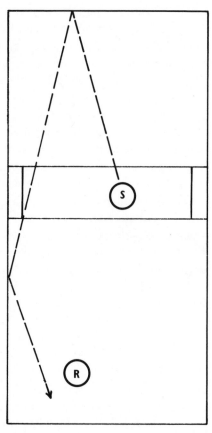

Illus. 63. The angle serve.

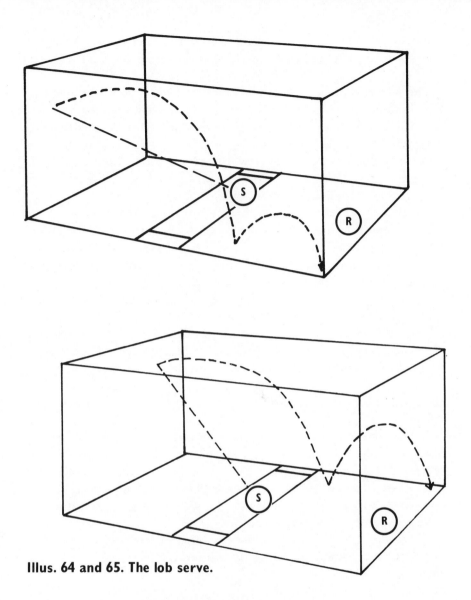

Illus. 64 and 65. The lob serve.

The Lob Serve

The lob serve is the opposite of the power serve. It is a graceful serve that is hit softly high on the front wall and rebounds at an angle in a high floating arc to a back corner of the court (Illus. 64-65). It is a very effective serve when hit near or slightly brushing the side wall. Slightly touching the side wall causes the ball to slow down and literally "die" in the backcourt and even if it doesn't, your opponent's swing will be slow and hesitant for fear of hitting the wall with his racquet.

This serve is mainly used as a change of pace. It is employed to change the tempo of play and is especially effective against an inexperienced, overanxious or overly aggressive player who tries to keep the game moving at a fast pace. The lob serve can also be used to neutralize a player who has a powerful offense. The flight of the ball in relation to the side wall causes the power hitters to wait and slow their swing, thus changing their style of play.

Another important function of the lob serve is its use as a second serve. When the first serve is not good, it is extremely important to get the next serve in or a loss of serve will result. It is also very important to serve the ball effectively or it is highly probable that you will lose your serve on your opponent's strong return. Developing a good second serve, then, is of prime importance. A well-executed lob serve can serve that purpose well.

The potency of the lob serve is often overlooked. The slow speed of the ball makes it look very easy to return. But when hit correctly, it forces your opponent to the rear of the court and allows you time to gain center-court position (see Chapter 8—*Strategy*). It also enables you to conserve energy because it doesn't require a powerful stroke.

To execute this serve, concentrate on hitting the ball high on the front wall and with only enough power for it to travel deep in the court and "die." This takes practice and concentration. If you do not concentrate, the lazy nature and ease of execution of this serve will tend to make you complacent and you will serve poorly, setting up your opponent for an easy return.

There are two types of lob serves—the underhand lob and the overhand lob. When hit correctly, either can be a very effective weapon.

THE UNDERHAND LOB SERVE

Of the two lob serves, the underhand lob is the one that is used more often as it is easier to perform and control than the overhand lob serve.

The underhand lob serve is usually executed from the forehand side using either an underhand or sidearm motion. To hit an underhand lob serve, grasp the racquet with a forehand grip and take a position near the center of the service zone. This will enable you to serve the ball to either side of the court. Stand in a relaxed manner

Illus. 66

Move your racquet arm to a position waist-high or higher . . . as the ball bounces, step forward with the front foot.

Illus. 67.

facing the front wall. Your feet should be spread comfortably apart with the foot opposite the racquet arm positioned slightly in front of the other. The body weight is over the rear foot and the knees and hips are flexed.

Hold the ball in your non-racquet hand slightly away from your body at a level somewhere between your knees and waist. The height at which the ball is held will be determined by comfort and control in dropping the ball and timing the hit. Move your racquet arm to a position waist-high or higher in back of your body with your elbow slightly flexed, wrist cocked and the racquet head tilted upward (Illus. 66).

Drop the ball to the floor, and as it bounces, step forward with the front foot and start the racquet arm moving forward (Illus. 67). During the forward swing, shift your weight from the rear to the front foot (Illus. 68). Time your swing to contact the ball near or slightly in front of the forward foot and at the top of the bounce. At the moment the ball is hit, the arm is fully extended and the wrist snapped gently (Illus. 69). This will send the ball softly toward the front wall.

After the ball is hit, the racquet continues forward and up (Illus. 70). This kind of follow-through will enable the ball to travel upward and hit high on the front wall. The swing eventually ends at a position about shoulder high on the opposite side of your body (Illus. 71).

Illus. 69.

Illus. 68.

Shift your weight from the rear to the front foot . . . extend the arm fully and snap the wrist gently at impact.

The racquet continues forward and up
. . . the swing ends at a position about
shoulder-high.

Illus. 70.

Illus. 71.

THE OVERHAND LOB SERVE

The overhand lob serve, although rarely used, is another variation that some players prefer. It is more difficult to execute but serves the same purpose as the underhand lob.

To perform the overhand lob serve, hold the racquet with a forehand grip. Stand erect in the middle of the service zone facing the front wall with your feet comfortably spread. One foot should be slightly in front of the other and your body weight over the back foot.

63

Illus. 72. Let your arms hang loosely along the sides of your body.

Illus. 73. Start the bounce high over your head.

Bend your knees slightly and let your arms hang loosely along the sides of your body (Illus. 72).

Begin the serve by bouncing the ball so that it rebounds from the floor high over your head (Illus. 73-76). This allows you to hit the ball about 6 to 12 inches in front of your head over the shoulder of your racquet arm. As you bounce the ball, move your racquet arm to a position behind the body similar to throwing a baseball overhand. In this position, your wrist should be cocked and your elbow bent with your body tilted slightly backward at the waist.

Begin your forward swing by pushing off the rear foot, stepping

Illus. 75.

Illus. 74.

The high bounce allows you to hit the ball about 6 to 12 inches in front of your head.

toward the ball and shifting your body weight forward to the front foot (Illus. 77). Simultaneously, swing your racquet forward and upward to meet the ball. At the moment of impact, your arm should be fully extended, your racquet held firmly and your wrist snapped gently (Illus. 78). Hit the ball with only enough force for it to strike high on the front wall and rebound deep into the backcourt, similar to the underhand lob serve.

Your racquet continues forward after hitting the ball and then sweeps down to a position on the opposite side of your body near the waist. This type of follow-through gives you better control over the serve.

Illus. 77.

Illus. 76.

Push off the rear foot and step toward the ball, shifting your weight to the front foot.

Illus. 78. At the moment of impact your arm should be fully extended.

The "Z" Serve

The "Z" serve is a crosscourt angle serve. It can be performed using any of the basic strokes and at varying speeds. When hit forcefully, it is called a *power "Z"* and if hit gently a *soft* or *half-lob "Z."*

The serve gets its name from the path of the ball as it travels around the court. It is designed so the ball rebounds from either front corner of the court to a position diagonally across the court. When the ball is served from the left side of the service zone, the flight of the served ball forms the letter "Z." If served from the right side, the path of the ball looks like an inverted "Z."

In a "Z" serve, the ball contacts the front wall near the side wall, angles sharply to the side wall and then travels crosscourt, bouncing on the floor behind the short line before hitting the opposite side wall (Illus. 79 and 80). Upon hitting the side wall, the ball spins violently causing it to rebound parallel to the back wall. This spinning action occurs more dramatically in the power "Z" than in the soft "Z." In the soft "Z," the ball does not rebound as sharply and angles toward the rear wall instead of parallel to it.

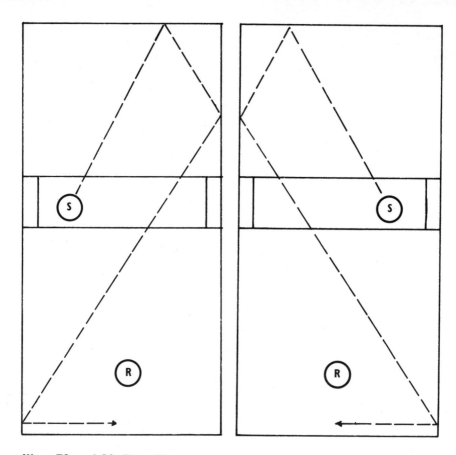

Illus. 79 and 80. The "Z" serve.

To execute either of the "Z" serves, stand a little off-center in the serving zone facing the side wall. Point the shoulder of the non-hitting arm toward the front corner of the wall in the intended direction the ball will initially travel. The stroking and body motion are similar to the movements for the power or lob serves, depending on whether you want to hit a power or soft "Z" serve.

The "Z" serve is an effective and deceptive serve, especially when hit with power and mixed with power serves. The initial motion of the ball tends to influence the receiver to move in the same direction the ball is first hit, even though it will eventually end up on the opposite side of the court. This serve is extremely effective when hit so the ball bounces deep in the court and rebounds parallel and close to or even slides along the back wall. The "Z" serve is the one primarily employed against right-handed players while the inverted "Z" is utilized against left-handed players. When used in either manner, the ball will be hit to the receiver's backhand side. Occasionally, the direction of the serve can and should be reversed to keep your opponent guessing and off-balance.

When hitting a "Z" serve, make sure you hit the ball with enough force and good placement to prevent the receiver from easily returning it. Also, be very careful not to hit the side wall first or have the rebound from the front wall hit you, as either will cause a loss of service. Finally, after serving the ball, move quickly to the center-court position (see Chapter 8—*Strategy*). If you do not move fast enough, you will be caught out of position when your opponent returns the ball, making your task of retrieving the next shot even more difficult.

The Slow Drive Serve

The slow drive serve is a half-speed serve that is commonly referred to as a *junk* or *garbage* serve. The ball is hit with medium force and travels the court in the same direction as the power serve. Although the ball is hit softly in this serve, it can be very difficult to return. The ball looks easy to hit and the receiver believes he is set

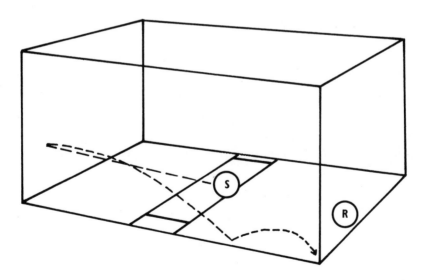

Illus. 81. The slow drive serve.

up for a kill shot return. Since the return looks easy, the receiver often becomes overanxious and hits the ball into the floor or tries to return the ball with too much power giving you an easy set-up off the back wall.

It is an excellent serve to use—very little energy is needed to perform it and the ball can be hit to a safe position on the court. This serve is even more effective when used as a change of pace serve in combination with the power serves. The change of speed can affect your opponent in such a way that the ball will be either over- or under-hit, resulting in an error.

The same basic techniques used for the power serve are employed when hitting the slow drive. The ball is served from the forehand side and contacted at about waist level. It travels to the front wall, striking it between 4 and 6 feet from the floor, then rebounds and strikes the floor just beyond the short line. It bounces deep into the court where it slows down and drops to the floor a second time before hitting the back wall (Illus. 81). The depth and speed of the ball add to the difficulty of returning the serve. Remember not to hit it too high or with too much force or it will rebound off the rear wall for an easy set-up for your opponent.

Serving Pointers

• Make sure your opponent is ready and your partner is in the doubles box before serving.

• Serve the ball with an objective in mind—don't serve just to put the ball in play.

• Evaluate your opponent's weakness and serve to it.

• Vary the height, speed and direction of the ball.

• Try to use the same stance and swing for all serves to avoid tipping off your opponent.

• Do not hurry the serve.

• Never commit an out serve—always make sure your serves are in play.

6. Receiving and Returning the Serve

Returning the serve is an extremely important facet of racquetball play—as important as knowing how to serve effectively. If you cannot return the serve well, you will always be on the defensive and probably lose the match since only the server can score points.

The main objective of the service return is to hit an offensive shot to win the serve or a defensive one to at least neutralize the server and place him on the defensive. It is important to know when to take the initiative and hit an offensive shot and when to play a defensive one. A good rule to follow is to return all shots above the knees defensively and those below the knees offensively. Further, the offensive shots should only be taken if you are in a good position to return the ball. If you have to hurry and rush your shot, then a defensive shot is in order even if the ball is below knee level.

There are six possible shots that can be utilized in returning the serve. They are the ceiling ball, the "Z" ball, the around-the-wall, the lob, the pass, and the kill shot. The first four are defensive shots and the latter two are offensive.

To retrieve and return the served ball successfully, you must first be able to move into position to hit it. Assuming the proper court position while waiting for the serve is the first step in getting to the ball.

The server has a distinct advantage over the receiver. Only the server knows when, where and how the serve will be hit. He also has the advantage of being able to serve the ball anywhere in the court behind the short line, this large an area representing half of the total playing area. The receiver on the other hand can only guess which serve will come his way and react to the ball after it is served. Since the receiver is at a disadvantage, it is important that he find the most advantageous receiving position.

The best receiving position that a receiver can take while waiting for the serve is the one that allows him to get into position to return the ball regardless of where it is served. This position is usually determined after evaluating both your opponent's and your own strengths and weaknesses. Court positions for receiving the serve in singles and doubles play will be discussed in depth in Chapter 8— *Strategy*.

Defensive Returns

THE CEILING RETURN

The ceiling shot return is the safest of all the defensive service returns. You can hit this shot so that the ball strikes the ceiling either before or after it hits the front wall. The first way, the ball is struck so that it hits high on the front wall, strikes the ceiling, lands midway in the backcourt, and bounces deep, preferably into a corner. The second way, the ball first strikes the ceiling a few feet before the front wall, bounces off the front wall, onto the floor, and then high and deep into the backcourt. Either way, the ball should be hit so the rebound hugs a side wall and travels toward your opponent's backhand.

Since the ball is high in the air through most of its flight, your opponent will have no choice but to move deep into the backcourt for a return. In this manner, you can neutralize his offensive shot and move to an offensive position on the court forcing him to move to a defensive one.

The ceiling return can be employed to return all of the various racquetball serves from the power serve to the lob. This shot will be dealt with in more detail on page 85.

THE "Z" BALL RETURN

The "Z" ball return, although used infrequently, is another effective way to return the serve. The path followed by the ball is the same as that of the "Z" serve (page 67), and will be discussed further in the section on the "Z" shot (page 92).

This return is not used very often because of the angle and difficulty required to hit it properly from deep in the court. To execute it correctly, you must hit the ball high and at the proper angle, otherwise it can be cut off by your opponent for an easy return. When hit correctly, the ball moves in crazy angles around the court and eventually dies in the backcourt area. Learn to use this shot; it will add another dimension to your game.

THE AROUND-THE-WALL RETURN

The around-the-wall return strikes first a side wall, then the front wall, then the other side wall, and travels across to the opposite rear corner. It is a risky defensive maneuver, one of the easiest defensive shots to return by the server. This shot is utilized mainly in doubles and singles play as a change of pace, or against an inexperienced player. Do not rely on it as your main defensive weapon. For more information, read about the around-the-wall shot on page 89.

THE LOB RETURN

This return is the same in principle as the lob serve (page 59). It is probably the easiest of the defensive shots for the server to return and is only utilized as a last resort when you cannot hit any of the other returns. For this shot to be effective, it must be hit high and soft in order to hug the side wall or travel crosscourt over your opponent's head. The ball will then contact the side wall deep in the court causing it to die. Sometimes players who lack the strength to hit a ceiling ball will use this type of return because it requires less energy to hit. This shot is explained in more detail on page 88.

Offensive Returns

THE PASS RETURN

The pass shot is the safer of the two offensive returns. Next to the ceiling return, it is the most widely used service return. This shot packs some offensive punch into your service return by placing you on the offensive from your first shot. Grabbing the offensive immediately puts more pressure on the server. There are two types of pass shot returns that are frequently used—the alley, or wall, pass and the crosscourt pass. They both have the same purpose—to go by the server (who is in the center of the court) out of his reach and die in the backcourt.

The more effective of the two, although harder to perform, is the alley, or wall, pass. The ball is hit from a position near one of the side walls. It travels straight to the front wall and bounces to the backcourt on a straight path close and parallel to the side wall (the same side wall from which you hit the shot). When hit correctly, this pass gives the server less time to rest and react before the ball has to be played. The ball travels the shortest distance in a straight line to and from the front wall in the shortest amount of time.

On the other hand, the crosscourt pass is easier to execute since you do not have to worry as much about the ball hitting the side wall. Like the alley pass, the crosscourt pass is hit near a side wall. But unlike the alley pass, the ball strikes the front wall at an angle and passes the server to the side opposite that from which it was hit. For example, if you hit the shot from near the right side wall, it angles off the front wall and passes the server on his left. The only danger is that this shot is usually directed towards the opponent's forehand. If the ball is not hit hard enough at the correct angle, your opponent will have a chance to cut it off in the front court and return it quickly into the right corner before you can cover that area.

Both of the pass shots should be hit hard and low or the ball will rebound off the rear wall for an easy set-up. The techniques used to execute the pass shots are discussed on pages 77 (alley pass) and 79 (crosscourt pass).

THE KILL SHOT RETURN

The kill shot is the most spectacular of the returns. It is used primarily to return weak serves and service set-ups. The kill shot strikes the front wall very close to the floor. It bounces low and short, making it very hard to return. This shot should not be used on all service returns because it's difficult to execute properly and the percentages are against you. If you miss it completely, the server scores a point or if you hit it too high, your opponent is in the front court area in a position to make an offensive return.

The kill return should be used wisely. It's a good idea to attempt kill returns at least occasionally in order to keep your opponent "honest." If you invariably return serves to the backcourt, the server will come to expect this and drop back after serving, thus cutting down the effectiveness of a deep return. A kill shot every now and then will force him to play closer to the front wall, giving you a better chance to hit an effective pass or lob. You can also use the kill return when your skill level is significantly better than your opponent's because you can take more chances. Finally, it can be utilized as a last resort, a go-for-broke measure if you are overly tired or your opponent's skill is so much better that you need to hit a kill to win the serve.

The different types of kill shots and how to execute them are described on pages 80-85.

Returning the Serve Pointers

- Assume the ready position and stand alertly facing the front wall.

- Be sure that your position on the court enables you to reach and return all possible serves; do not overplay one side of the court.

- Generally, return all shots above the waist with a defensive return and hit all shots below the waist with an offensive return.

- Return weak returns with a kill shot or other offensive return.

- Vary your returns—do not become predictable.

- After returning the serve, more quickly to the center-court position.

- Always keep your eyes on the ball, but use your peripheral vision to keep track of your opponent.

7. The Shots

Once you master the technique of moving to the ball and hitting it correctly, you must learn when and where to hit the ball. A successful racquetball player knows how to do this. He can automatically select the proper stroke to use in hitting the correct shot in any given situation.

There are seven basic shots in racquetball. They are the pass, the kill, the drop, the ceiling ball, the lob, the "Z," and the around-the-wall ball. The first three are offensive shots and the latter four defensive. Each of these shots should be practiced until it can be performed automatically. Being able to select and execute the correct shot without having to think about it will leave your mind free to concentrate on strategy.

The Pass Shot

The pass is an offensive shot and probably the most frequently used of all the basic shots. As the name implies, the objective of the shot is to hit the ball so it passes out of the reach of your opponent and cannot be retrieved.

This shot is relatively easy to perform and can be hit with any of the basic strokes—forehand, backhand, overhand or underhand. In a properly-executed pass shot, the ball should contact the front wall about 3 feet from the floor. It should be hit with enough power to drive it past your opponent, not too hard or too high, or it will rebound off the back wall and into the middle of the court for an easy set-up.

The pass shot can be hit to either side of the court. The placing, timing, and type of pass shot used is determined by your opponent's weaknesses and position on the court. There is relatively little risk in this shot—it is a high percentage shot and allows lots of room for error. The pass is a safer offensive shot than the kill because the ball hits higher on the front wall, reducing the number of balls hitting the floor and thus resulting in fewer errors.

Although a well-executed pass will usually win a point, it is not always necessary to hit it perfectly to score or gain an advantage. A fairly good shot may not score, but will at least force your opponent to chase after the ball and vacate the center-court position.

When executing a pass shot, remember to watch the ball, turn your body sideways, rotate your hips and shoulders, step into the ball, snap your wrist, and follow through.

In addition to speed, direction and control also contribute to a successful shot. These components should also be considered when practicing the pass shot using the drills found in Chapter 9.

There are several variations of the pass shot. They are the wall, or alley, pass; the angle pass; and the crosscourt, or "V," pass. It is important to learn all of them because each is an effective method of scoring or neutralizing an opponent.

THE ALLEY PASS

In this shot (sometimes referred to as the wall pass or the down-the-line pass), the ball is hit so that it rebounds from the front wall and travels down the alley to the rear wall on a path parallel to the side wall (Illus. 82). The alley of the court is an imaginary area near each side wall, 18 inches wide (the width of the doubles service boxes). The closer the path of the ball to the side wall, the harder it will be to return.

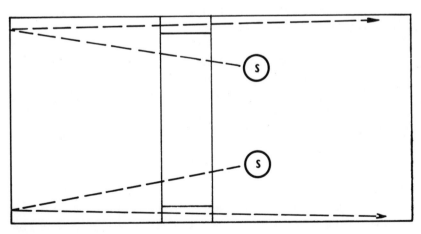

Illus. 82. The alley pass.

This shot is usually hit when you are in the center of the court and your opponent is positioned to either side of the court. It is hit down the alley near the side wall and is most effective when your body is between the ball and your opponent (Illus. 83). A shot from this position will momentarily delay your opponent, as he has to pick up the flight of the ball before he can move into position to hit it.

Illus. 83. The alley pass is most effective when your body is between the ball and your opponent.

An experienced opponent, when caught out of position, will often anticipate this shot. As you hit the shot, he will move toward the side to which the ball is to be hit. If a player is consistently overanticipating and getting into good position to return this shot, try to feint one way when hitting the ball and then hit it in the other direction down the alley that your opponent has left open. This will catch him off guard and moving the wrong way. Eventually, it will force your opponent to stay in position and will make your shots more effective.

THE ANGLE PASS

Another variation of the pass shot is the angle pass. In this shot, the ball hits approximately 2 to 4 feet from the floor on the front wall and angles to the side wall without bouncing on the floor. The ball then caroms off the side wall toward the backcourt (Illus. 84).

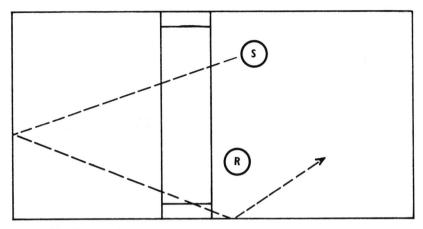

Illus. 84. The angle pass.

To be effective, the ball should be hit with sufficient force to carry it to the side wall before your opponent can hit it in order to prevent him from making a return in the front-court. However, the ball should not be hit so hard or high that it reaches the back wall before it bounces twice. The ball should also strike the side wall on the same side your opponent is standing at a spot even with or beyond his court position.

The main objective of this shot is to force your opponent to initially react and chase the ball to one side of the court only to have the ball rebound to the other side. This shot is very effective when used in sequence with the alley pass and when your opponent is positioned at or in front of the short line.

THE CROSSCOURT PASS

The crosscourt pass, or "V" shot, is another of the pass shots that is frequently used during play. When hit correctly, the ball strikes low on the front wall and angles away from your opponent. Exactly where the ball should contact the front wall will depend upon your opponent's court position. Generally it should hit near the middle part of the wall (Illus. 85).

This shot is most effective if performed when your opponent is deep or to one side of the court. It should be hit low and away from him. The speed, height and angle of the ball are important to the success of this shot. If the ball is hit too slowly, too high or at an incorrect angle, the shot will be easily returned.

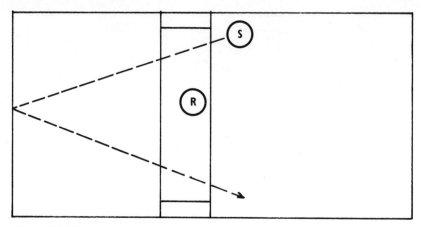

Illus. 85. The crosscourt pass.

The Kill Shot

The most spectacular and colorful of all the basic racquetball shots is the kill shot. It is akin to the smash in tennis, the bomb in football and the home run in baseball. This shot provides a flair to the game—it overwhelms the opposition and is exciting for the spectator to watch. The main objective in hitting a kill shot is to strike the ball in such a way that it hits and rebounds from the front wall very close to the floor making it practically impossible to retrieve.

There are three variations of the kill shot—the straight or front-wall kill, the pinch or corner kill, and the fly kill. It is important to learn how and when to execute them all so that you can include them in your arsenal of shots; each is effective in its own way and in different situations.

When attempting a kill shot, watch the ball and assume a good hitting stance. Let the ball drop as low as possible before striking it. Hit the ball only after it drops below your waist and preferably below your knees. Ideally, the ball should be contacted when it is approximately ankle-high (Illus. 86).

To hit the ball correctly, assume a low body position by bending at the knees and waist. This allows you to lower the racquet to meet the ball. All the other basic techniques that are fundamental to efficient strokes apply to the kill. These include turning the body sideways, rotating the shoulders and hips, stepping to meet the ball, using a full arm swing, snapping the wrist, and following-through after the shot. Each one of these components is essential and contributes to executing a powerful kill.

Illus. 86. Striking the ball in a kill shot.

The kill shot is hit with either a sidearm or underhand stroke. The choice of stroke used will depend upon your skill level, your body position, and your position on the court. Rarely is an overhand stroke employed to hit a kill. The majority of kill shots attempted from a high position either result in a missed shot or a set-up as it is hard to successfully angle the ball down to hit low on the front wall without striking the floor first. Besides, no matter how low you hit the front wall, the ball will rebound upward because of the angle and will give your opponent an opportunity to retrieve the ball. The best chance for an overhand kill is to hit the ball so that it contacts two walls. That is, the ball should contact the front wall and a side wall near the corner of the court.

Kill shots can be hit from almost any position on the court. However, they are most successful when executed from the front-court, especially when your opponent is positioned in back of you, to the side of you, or is off-balance.

The effectiveness of the kill shot depends on the low trajectory of the ball and its accurate placement. These components, together with the distance your opponent must travel to try and retrieve it, make the task of returning the ball very difficult. If you are on the receiving end of a correctly hit kill shot, there is very little that you can do to retrieve it. Your only hope is to pray that you are in good enough position to at least have an opportunity to try to dig it out. However, unless this shot is not hit well, you will have very little chance of returning it successfully.

To learn how and when to hit good kill shots requires lots of patience and practice. Although experience plays a part in developing the timing and skill necessary to hit kill shots, much of it comes through long hours of practice. The drills presented in Chapter 9 of this book are an excellent means to help you develop and perfect your kill shot arsenal.

THE STRAIGHT KILL

The straight, or front-wall, kill simply hits and rebounds from the front wall in a straight line (Illus. 87). This makes it the easiest of all the kill shots to learn and the easiest to defend against. This shot is employed most effectively when hit near a side wall or in a line away from where your opponent is positioned.

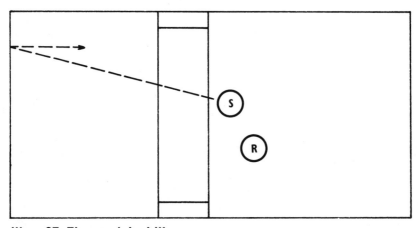

Illus. 87. The straight kill.

THE CORNER KILL

The most effective of the kill shots is the corner, or pinch, kill. It is also called a two-wall kill for reasons soon to be obvious. There are two variations of the corner kill—the side-wall-front-wall and the front-wall-side-wall shots. The names of the shots reflect the action of the ball as it contacts the walls.

The side-wall-front-wall kill shot is sometimes referred to as an outside corner kill. In this shot the ball hits the side wall first, then rebounds to the front wall and angles sharply toward the opposite side wall (Illus. 88).

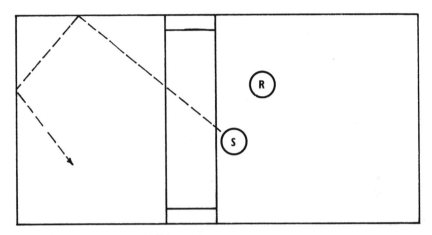

Illus. 88. The corner kill.

Of the two corner kill shots, this one is the most effective because the ball angles downward after striking the side wall causing it to hit low on the front wall and making it hard to retrieve. The low rebound of the ball is helped by the spin imparted on it after it hits the side wall. This is an important point to remember because it allows a player to hit the ball a little higher on the side wall and still make a successful kill shot.

The side-wall-front-wall kill shot is an excellent shot to employ when your opponent is trapped out of position near a side wall. When this occurs, the ball should be hit so that it contacts the side wall closest to your opponent. It will then angle off to the front wall and rebound away from your opponent.

When used in sequence with an alley pass, it can be even more effective. The pass sets up the kill shot by forcing your opponent to retrieve the ball near a side wall. If your opponent's return is weak then you will have an easy set-up for the kill.

Against right-handed players, the right side-wall-front-wall kill is very effective because the ball angles away from the player to his backhand side, which is generally his weak side. The reverse is true for left-handed players; the left side-wall-front-wall kill is more effective.

In the front-wall-side-wall kill shot, also known as the inside corner kill, the ball hits the front wall first and then the side wall (Illus. 89). It is not as effective as the side-wall-front-wall kill shot because the ball bounces higher off the floor on the return from the front wall due to the opposite spin generated. It also rebounds toward the center of the court in the direction of your opponent. These two factors make it easier to return.

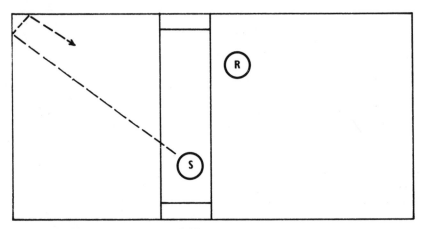

Illus. 89. The inside corner kill.

For this kill shot to be effective, the ball must be hit low and accurately or your opponent will be in a position to successfully return the ball. The shot should only be attempted when your opponent is either out of position or deep in the court.

THE FLY KILL SHOT

The fly kill shot is one of the most aggressive and devastating shots in racquetball play. It is a very effective shot and is used to quicken the pace of a rally, maintain the center-court position, and keep an opponent running and off-balance. Executing this shot also allows an opponent less time to rest or get set and into position between shots. Although the fly kill shot is an extremely effective weapon, few people use and capitalize on it because it is one of the hardest shots to learn and master.

To execute the fly kill shot correctly requires split-second reaction, good judgment, precise timing, and lots of practice. The basic form for executing a fly kill is the same as the kill shots described previously with the main difference being that the ball is contacted in mid-air prior to its first bounce. The ball should be contacted as low as possible, preferably below knee level. To insure that the point of contact is low, players must bend both at the waist and knees.

Learning this shot depends on the ability of a player to gauge the speed and path of the rebound of the ball from the previous shot and to move swiftly into position to hit it. This may require a player to move forward to cut the ball off or even backward to allow the ball to drop as low as possible before striking it.

Any of the various kill shots previously described can be executed from the fly kill hitting position. This shot can also be performed from almost any position on the court, either on the forehand or backhand side, and employing any of the racquetball strokes—overhand, sidearm or underhand.

Before attempting this shot, compare it to the regular kill shot. Note the similarities and differences between the two shots. Remember, when executing this shot:
- Stay low.
- Watch the ball.
- Move quickly into the hitting position.
- Contact the ball as low as possible.

The fly kill is most effectively used during a rally when executed from a position in the middle of the court or closer to the front wall, either after a weak return of serve or shot from deep in the backcourt. The suddenness of execution tends to catch an opponent by surprise and off-guard. Thus, because of the element of surprise, a perfectly executed shot is not always necessary for a winner. However, do not get complacent when hitting a fly kill shot or you will miss it or find yourself on the defensive because your opponent made a good recovery and was able to return it.

The Ceiling Shot

The ceiling shot is the main defensive shot and perhaps the safest shot in racquetball and its role has become significantly more important as the ball has gotten livelier. This shot is primarily a neutralizing shot used to move your opponent from the center-court position. When hit correctly, your opponent will have a hard time returning it with anything other than another defensive shot, probably another ceiling ball.

The ceiling ball is similar in purpose to the lob in tennis and the clear in badminton. It is used to change the tempo of play by making your opponent chase the ball to the backcourt. This shot also gives you added time to rest between shots because of the time it takes for the ball to travel the court and allows you to regain control of the center-court area. This is crucial, as you will see in Chapter 8—*Strategy*. The opportunity to rest during play is especially important to those players who are not as physically fit as they should be or when there is an extended rally causing the players to fatigue rapidly. A well-hit ceiling shot can even force an error from an opponent if he cannot return it or mishits it and sets you up for a kill. It is an excellent shot to use for a player who has lots of control in order for him to neutralize the effects of a power shooter. Slowing down the tempo of play can be unnerving to a power hitter.

The overhand stroke is generally used for the ceiling shot. The forehand is probably the easiest to learn and to use, while the overhand-backhand ceiling shot is perhaps the most difficult to execute and requires a great deal of practice to master. To hit a ceiling shot, the ball must be hit with enough force to enable it to travel deep in the court. It should not be hit too hard or it will rebound from the rear wall for an easy return. How hard the ball is hit will depend to a great degree on the liveliness of the ball. When warming up prior to play, you should test the ball by hitting several ceiling shots.

Usually, the ceiling shot is contacted when the ball is above shoulder height. The ball is hit so it goes directly to the ceiling, approximately one to four feet from the front wall. After striking the ceiling, the ball angles sharply to the front wall and then to the floor in the front-court. It then bounces very high into the air and travels deep into the backcourt near the rear wall (Illus. 90). If the shot is well

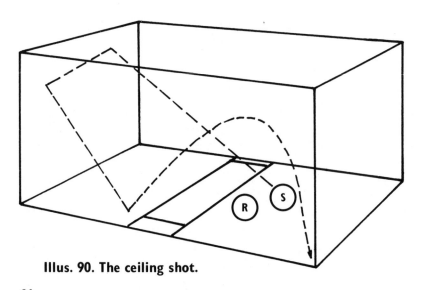

Illus. 90. The ceiling shot.

executed, it will be difficult to play after hitting the floor or the back wall. This shot will be even more difficult to return when hit to a player's weak side—usually the backhand.

Another variation of the ceiling shot is the front-wall-ceiling ball. In this shot, the ball hits the front wall first and then the ceiling about midway back in the court. After hitting the ceiling, the ball drops directly to the floor and bounces toward the back wall (Illus. 91). The spin generated by this shot is directly opposite that of the ceiling-front wall shot. The ball picks up backspin, causing it to slow down and die in the backcourt even before reaching the back wall. It is important that the ball contact the ceiling after hitting the front wall, or it will strike high on the back wall, setting up your opponent for a very easy return.

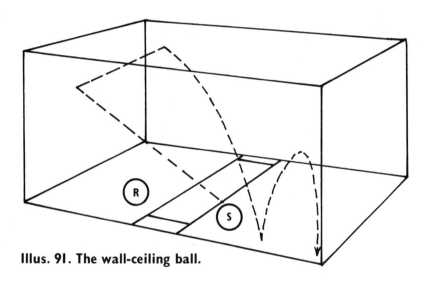

Illus. 91. The wall-ceiling ball.

All the fundamentals employed to hit the overhand stroke previously described are used to execute the ceiling shot. Position yourself so that you can contact the ball above your shoulders and slightly in front of your body. Then shift your weight over the rear foot and bring your racquet arm behind your body as if you were throwing a football. The elbow of the racquet arm is bent, the wrist cocked and the racquet tilted downwards. Next, start the swing by pushing off the rear foot, transferring the weight forward and stepping toward the ball. At the same time swing your racquet forward to contact the ball, snap your wrist and then follow through.

When hitting the front wall-ceiling ball, you can also use an underhand stroke. It is easier to hit the ball at an angle so it will contact the ceiling after striking the front wall. Occasionally this stroke can also be used to hit the ceiling-front wall shot. If you use an underhand stroke, make sure that you employ all the basics of the underhand stroke. Follow through in a forward and upward arc with the racquet coming to a stop above your shoulder.

Since the ceiling shot is probably the most effective defensive shot in the game, it should be practiced until it is mastered. Once it is perfected, it will allow you to play the percentages instead of always trying to hit the ball hard even from awkward positions on the court.

The Lob Shot

In the formative years of racquetball, the lob was considered a very important defensive shot to move your opponent from the center-court position. Today, with the introduction of the "live" ball, this shot has taken a back seat to the ceiling ball and even the "Z" shot. Although the lob is rarely used, it is important to understand its characteristics and functions—you may have an opportunity to use it occasionally or even have it used against you.

The lob is a high, soft, floating shot that travels deep in the court similar to the lob serve. It is used at times when you want to keep the ball in play rather than risk a difficult or impossible shot.

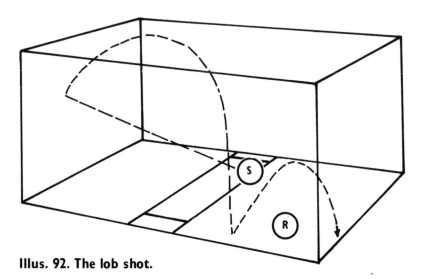

Illus. 92. The lob shot.

To execute a lob, you can use any of the basic strokes. The stroke you use will depend on your court position and the flight of the ball. This shot may be hit with only a flick of the wrist and virtually no follow-through, making it especially useful when you are caught out of position and have very little time to play the ball. For the lob to be successful, the ball must be hit high over your opponent's head near a side wall. It may also be hit crosscourt so the ball just barely contacts the side wall deep in the court. When the ball is hit in this way, it will slow down and die in the backcourt, making the return difficult (Illus. 92). It should be pointed out that this is a very risky and difficult shot to hit. If the ball is hit too short or too long or not close enough to a side wall, it will result in an easy set-up for your opponent.

The Around-the-Wall Shot

The around-the-wall shot is a three-wall shot; like the other defensive shots, it is designed to move your opponent from the center-court area to a position deep in the backcourt. This is a secondary defensive shot and is not as effective as the "Z" because the ball does not behave as erratically after striking the third wall, thus making it easier to return. It is more effectively utilized in doubles than singles play.

The around-the-wall shot can be hit with a forehand, backhand or overhand stroke. It is usually executed from deep in the court when the ball is above your waist and you cannot use any of the other defensive shots because you are out of position or running after the ball.

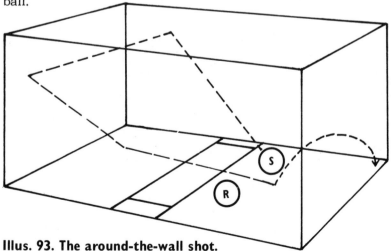

Illus. 93. The around-the-wall shot.

To perform the around-the-wall shot, hit the ball so it strikes the side wall first, then the front wall and finally the other side wall. The ball then angles crosscourt to the opposite rear corner of the court (Illus. 93). The ball should be hit firmly and high so it travels deep into the court. If the ball is hit low or too deep it will result in an easy set-up for your opponent. Perfecting this shot is very difficult, but you should try to learn it or at least know that it exists. You may have an occasion to use it to keep the ball in play.

The Drop Shot

A drop shot is a "finesse" shot that requires good timing and racquet control to execute. It is most successful when hit from the front-court while your opponent is in the back quarter of the court.

The shot can be hit with a forehand, backhand or underhand stroke; it can be hit in a straight line or angled crosscourt. When executing a drop shot, hit the ball softly and delicately so that it barely contacts the front wall. The shot should be hit low (Illus. 94) so the rebound touches the floor immediately after contacting the front wall. The combination of the ball hitting low, together with a very short rebound from the front wall, makes this shot very difficult to retrieve.

Deception in the execution of the drop shot can also add to your opponent's difficulty in returning it. A properly hit drop shot is disguised to resemble the other strokes. This way, you will make your opponent hold his position until the ball is actually hit, so he will have less time to run to retrieve the ball before it bounces a second time.

The appearance of the execution of a drop shot should be similar to the other strokes until just before you hit the ball. During the swing, slow the forward movement of your racquet arm and, at the moment of impact, relax the grip and wrist (Illus. 95). The racquet then pushes rather than swings the ball in the intended direction of the shot (Illus. 96). The pushing action and the relaxed grip and wrist tend to deaden the impact of the ball. The backswing can also be shortened to soften the shot. The racquet face can either be held squarely or slightly open, depending on your distance from the front wall and the angle of contact with the ball. Remember when executing a drop shot that "touch" or "finesse," not power, is the important ingredient to its successful execution.

Illus. 94.   Illus. 95.

The drop shot should be hit low . . . at
the moment of impact, relax the grip
and wrist . . . the racquet then pushes
rather than swings the ball.

Illus. 96.

The "Z" Shot

The "Z" shot, or "Z" ball as it is sometimes called, is a very effective three-wall defensive shot. The purpose of this shot is similar to the ceiling ball or the lob. It is used to move your opponent from center-court to a position deep in the court to retrieve the ball. By executing the "Z," you will also have more time to rest between shots and to regain control of the center-court area.

The "Z" can be hit from almost any area of the court with either a forehand, backhand or overhand stroke. Usually, it is hit when the ball is waist-high or above and you are positioned to one side of the court. This shot can be used interchangeably with the ceiling ball and the lob. It is especially useful when you want to hit the ball deep in the court from the front-court to gain time to get back into position to later return the ball with a more offensive shot.

When executed properly, the "Z" ball is hard to return. If the ball is hit high and deep, your opponent will either have to return the ball on the fly with an overhead shot or let the ball travel to the backcourt. When the ball is deep in the court, it is difficult to hit it squarely because the ball rebounds from the third wall and travels near the back wall. This makes it difficult to swing forcefully or to even get the racquet on the ball.

To execute a "Z" shot, hit the ball high into the opposite front corner of the court. It must be hit powerfully and contact the front

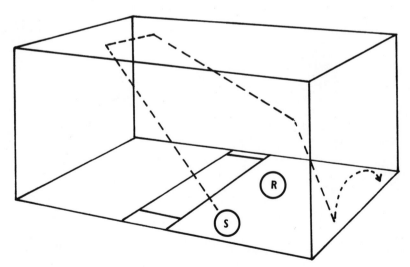

Illus. 97. The "Z" shot.

wall close to the side wall. The ball then angles sharply to the side wall and rebounds high and deep crosscourt to the opposite side wall in the backcourt without bouncing on the floor (Illus. 97). The spin created on the ball when it strikes the second side wall causes it to rebound parallel to the rear wall. If hit very deep in the court, the rebound of the ball may slide or hug the back wall making it extremely difficult to return. A well-executed "Z" shot will force a weak return or may even score a point.

The Back Wall Shot

A back wall shot is not really a shot *per se*, but actually the art of hitting the ball after it rebounds from the back wall. All of the basic racquetball shots and their variations can be executed off the rebound from the back wall. The two shots that are the most frequently used are the pass and the kill shots.

Theoretically speaking, this should be one of the easiest shots to perform because the ball and racquet are moving in the same direc-

Illus. 98 and 99. You must continually watch the flight of the ball as it approaches the back wall.

Illus. 100.　Illus. 101.

Pivot to follow the moving ball
...move your racquet to a position
waist-high behind your body ...
allow the ball to drop to knee-level.

Illus. 102.

94

tion. However, many players, especially beginners, experience difficulty in using it. They generally lack the instinct or experience to anticipate where the ball will rebound so they can execute a good shot, or they lack the patience to let the ball drop to the lowest possible point before hitting it. Once learned and mastered, the art of playing the ball off the back wall becomes the delight of the advanced player.

In attempting a back wall shot, you must continually watch the flight of the ball as it approaches the back wall (Illus. 98). As the ball passes you, pivot to follow the moving ball—never turn your back to it (Illus. 99 and 100). During the pivot, move your racquet to a position waist high behind your body (Illus. 101), the elbow of the racquet arm flexed and the wrist cocked.

As the ball rebounds off the rear wall, adjust your hitting position to allow the ball to drop below waist level, preferably to knee level, before contacting it (Illus. 102). This will be no problem if you are already in perfect position to hit the ball (Illus. 103–107). If you're not, use a two-step movement similar to the one employed in the two-step power serve (page 55).

Illus. 103 and 104. There will be no problem if you are in the perfect position to hit the ball as shown here.

Illus. 105.   Illus. 106.

Illus. 107.

Move your rear foot forward . . . hit
the ball as low as possible . . . the arm
swing continues forward as far and
low as possible.

First move your rear foot forward slightly, still keeping it behind your body, transferring your weight to this foot (Illus. 105). Then step into the shot, as much as possible toward the front wall, with the other leg. Time the steps and swing the racquet so that the ball will be hit as low as possible (Illus. 106).

At the moment of impact, snap your wrist to add more power to the shot. The arm swing continues forward as far and as low as possible to insure a low placement of the ball (Illus. 107). All of the basic stroking fundamentals are employed to execute the back wall shot.

BACK WALL POINTERS

• Always keep your eyes on the ball.

• Pivot in the same direction as the ball is passing on—never turn your back to the ball.

• Begin the backswing at the same time as the pivot.

• Adjust your body position to contact the ball as low as possible.

• Snap your wrist upon contact.

• Maintain a long, low follow-through.

• Remember all the basic fundamentals of stroking when performing this shot.

8. Strategy

Once you have learned to perform the racquetball skills and techniques efficiently and consistently, the next step is to learn and understand when and where to use them. In order to effectively utilize your skills to their maximum potential, you should have a game plan or plan of attack. This is the strategy that you employ against your opponent. How skillfully you can execute this plan will determine the outcome of the contest.

When developing your strategy, there are several components that should be considered and analyzed. They are as follows:

• Shot-making skills (your own and your opponent's).

• Physical condition and body build (your own and your opponent's).

• Pattern of play (your own and your opponent's).

• The court (lighting, construction, temperature and humidity).

Regardless of the kind of strategy you consider, you must adapt it to fit your own style of play. It should capitalize on your strengths, minimize your weaknesses and fit your physical make-up. Your strategy should also concentrate on attacking and taking advantage of your opponent's weaknesses while avoiding his strengths.

In General

The following factors should be considered in developing your strategy and tactics for racquetball. These factors are important regardless of whether you are playing singles, doubles, or cutthroat.

PRE-MATCH PLANNING

Before playing a match, you should have an intelligent game plan to use during the contest. The evaluation material presented in

Chapter 12 will help you do this. The Shot Analysis and Scouting Chart will provide you with information about your opponent's shot performance while the Racquetball Scorecard will give you information pertaining to your opponent's scoring pattern.

Other data you should be aware of are your opponent's age, body build and physical condition. Knowing these factors can give you a clue to the type of game and strategy your opponent will play. Then you can create a plan of attack to successfully combat it. For example, if your opponent is on the portly side with an excess of weight around the middle, you should hit the ball hard and low. When analyzing players having this type of physique, stamina and speed will be suspect. They will probably have difficulty moving to and retrieving low shots, especially ones that are angled away from them.

Tall and lean players generally are rangey and cover a lot of territory. These players are very difficult to pass. They seem to be able to retrieve any shot before it reaches the rear wall. Although these players are good ralliers, they usually have trouble turning quickly and returning shots that are hit powerfully below their knees.

Opponents who are short and thin are generally very agile and quick. Their vulnerability is the ceiling ball. They either have to wait until the ball rebounds off the rear wall to make the return or sometimes jump off the floor to return the shot. Either way, if the ceiling ball is hit correctly, they will probably have trouble making a good return.

Young racquetball players primarily rely on their speed afoot and fast reflexes. They like to play a fast and powerful game. These players also try to retrieve practically every shot, no matter how difficult it is. You can even see them diving to return a shot. They don't know when to quit! This over-anxiousness or anxiety to play at a fast tempo can be used against them. A smart player will slow down the tempo of play, which will in turn affect the other player's rhythm and possibly the outcome of the contest.

Older players like to control the tempo of the contest. They try to conserve their energy and use it wisely—no wasted motion or movement if possible. When playing an older opponent, speed up play by hitting more shots on the volley. Do not give this player an opportunity to rest. Always keep the game moving. Hit shots that will make him continually run to retrieve the ball.

After you have analyzed your opponent and developed your game plan, the next step is to implement it. Before you start the game, briefly review your plan. Once the game starts, make sure that you go by it. If your game plan is working successfully, stay with it. On the other hand, if it is not working, call a time out and try to quickly analyze why it is not working. Then change or modify it. Change your plan only if you are losing. Never, never, never change it if you are winning.

UNDERSTANDING THE COURT

You should thoroughly inspect the court prior to play. Having knowledge of the court conditions will help you in preparing and implementing your game plan.

When you inspect the court, check the lighting, the construction, the temperature, and the height of the rear wall. In addition, you should look for any obstructions on the court (such as transoms, temperature regulators, etc.) and proper closing and flushness of the entry door. All these factors can affect the rebound of the ball and the type of game you will play.

If the lighting is too dim or too bright, it will make it difficult for you to initially see the rebound of the ball. This may mean hitting hard and low shots if the lighting is dim or more ceiling shots if the lighting is too bright.

It is important to check the court temperature. When the court is hot and humid, or if there is a significant difference in temperature between the outdoor and indoor temperatures, or there is a lot of continuous play on the court, the wall and floor tend to become damp and wet. If you notice condensation forming, forget all your clever shots and concentrate on hitting the ball forcefully, low and into a wall. Under these circumstances, the ball will become "livelier" and bounce erratically. Instead of bouncing and rebounding in a normal manner, the ball will become wet and skid or slide on the rebound. The wetness on the court will also make the floor slippery and restrict the maneuverability of the players. The high humidity and heat may cause the participants to fatigue more quickly. On the other hand, courts with cooler temperatures cause the ball to slow down and allow players to utilize all the knowledge and skills they have at their command.

ANTICIPATION

In racquetball, anticipation is the ability to predict your opponent's forthcoming shot in order to move into a good position to return it. To anticipate correctly, you must learn and understand your opponent's moves. Once you can "read" the visual cues that a player sends out, you will be able to move quickly into position and prepare for the return.

The ability to anticipate correctly is usually achieved through experience and requires a detailed knowledge and understanding of the game and your opponent. Knowing what your opponent can and cannot do makes it easier to predict which shots he will execute. Information gleaned from the Shot Analysis and Scouting Chart will help you in this area. A thorough understanding of the game enables you to predict more accurately what shots can be used in certain situations and how the ball will rebound and react. This comes through practice and play, which teaches you when to react and prevents you from moving prematurely or too late. If you move too quickly, your opponent will switch shots and you will be caught either out of position or moving in the wrong direction. On the other hand, if you wait too long, you will be unable to move into position fast enough to make an effective return.

To learn to anticipate correctly you must recognize the perceptual cues your opponent provides you with. These cues will assist you in predicting the next shot. To help accomplish this, you must keep your eyes on the ball and still keep track of your opponent. You should especially notice his court position, foot position, the type of stroke he is using and the height at which the ball is played. These are some of the visual cues that will help tip off your opponent's intentions. A combination of all the above factors will make it easier for you to intelligently predict and prepare for your opponent's upcoming shot.

PERCENTAGE PLAY

Percentage play means selecting and hitting shots based on favorable odds or outcomes. Simply stated, it means hitting a shot in which you have an extremely good chance of winning the point or serve and only a very slight chance of your opponent retrieving or returning it effectively.

Playing the percentages can also mean cutting down or eliminating as many mistakes as possible. Frequently, the difference between a player winning or losing a match is the number of errors he makes. The player who makes the fewest errors generally wins the contest. By playing percentage racquetball, you will be able to reduce the number of errors you make. It will have a significant effect on the outcome of your matches.

During a contest, there are times when some shots are not as risky to execute as others. In these situations, always use the safer shot. For example, when given the choice of performing a highly risky shot (like a kill shot from deep court) and a safer shot (like the pass) to achieve the same result, select the safer shot which allows a larger margin of error. By selecting the pass over the kill in this situation, you are decreasing the possibility of committing an error and increasing your chances of success.

As you analyze and evaluate your past performances, you will become increasingly aware of the importance of reducing the number of errors you commit and playing the percentages. This even becomes more evident as you try to defeat more highly skilled players.

When playing the percentages, there are two factors that must be considered—serving and receiving. Obviously, you can gamble more or take unnecessary chances when you are serving. If you commit an error while serving, all you lose is the privilege of serving. On the other hand, a foolish mistake by a receiver results in a point for the server. As the server, the percentages to take a chance are in your favor. You can attempt more daring shots because you have a lot less to lose. But remember, you may try risky shots but not ridiculously foolish ones, or you will find yourself continually losing the serve without scoring many points.

As the receiver, you are on the defensive and in a poor situation percentage-wise. A costly mistake from this position will enable your opponent to score. The immediate task of the receiver is to gain the center-court position. This is accomplished by hitting one of the defensive shots, not to score, but to move your opponent to a defensive position on the court. Thus, your primary objective is to force an error or weak return so you can win the serve.

One of the keys to percentage play is to learn when to play offensively and when to play defensively. Too many players are only offense-minded when they should be playing defensively. To play defensively takes patience and good racquet control. It also means taking the offensive only when a good opportunity avails itself.

Playing the percentages also means hitting the shots primarily to your opponent's weaknesses and rarely to his strengths. This begins with the serve and continues into the rally. In doubles, this means serving and rallying mostly to the weaker of the two partners and rarely to the stronger player. The only time the ball should be hit to a player's or team's strength is to keep them honest and prevent them from overplaying and protecting their weaknesses.

Throughout the entire contest, keep your cool. Try and avoid the temptations of the poor percentage, high-risk shot even though it may look easy and very inviting to hit. Play the shot with the smallest chance for error. It will help increase the number of points you score each game.

SERVING THE BALL

Determine your opponent's weakness prior to serving the ball and hit your best serve to that area. By serving to your opponent's weakness, your serve will be more effective and achieve better results. In highly competitive tournament play, approximately 90 per cent of the serves are made to the opponent's weak side, usually the backhand. This gives the server an advantage and helps insure a weak return. Under certain conditions, however, a serve is directed to an opponent's strong side. This keeps your opponent honest and prevents him from overplaying a portion of the court to protect the weakness.

The factors that should be considered when determining which type of serve will achieve the best results are height, speed and the direction of the ball. It is essential to learn a variety of serves, to be able to control all three components of the serve. You do not know when you may have to change any one of these components to make your serve more effective. One set of factors may work well one day against a particular player, but might not work as well or at all the next day playing someone else.

Remember, it is important to develop a good serve to overcome and disguise other deficiencies or inadequacies you might have. This is often the determining factor between winning and losing. The serve is also the only shot in the game in which a player has the time to see the opponent's position on the court, the opportunity to determine which shot will be best, and the time to set up and execute it without having to run after the ball and hurry to hit it. This gives the server a decided advantage, but proper use of this advantage demands thought. Therefore, deliberate and calculated reasoning should go into planning and executing the serve. A good serve is the shortest road to successful play. (Also see the sections on the Serve, page 49; Serving Pointers, page 70; Serving in Singles, page 104; and Serving in Doubles, page 111.)

Singles Strategy

Strategy in singles competition requires an understanding of several aspects of play including serving, receiving the serve, returning the serve, court position and shot selection during a rally. Of course, it is assumed that you have learned to execute the skills necessary to implement game strategy. Once you have mastered the skills and have a thorough knowledge and understanding of how to use them, your chances of being successful are greatly increased.

SERVING IN SINGLES

The serve is of prime importance to success in singles. You should develop a good serve because it will place your opponent on the defensive from the onset of play. An effective serve will help you to establish an advantage that you can maintain throughout the entire game and match. For more information on how to serve, what constitutes an effective serve, and the different types of serves, read Chapter 5—*The Serve.*

When serving in singles, you should always serve the ball to your opponent's weak side—in the majority of cases, the backhand side. By serving the ball to the receiver's weakness, you have a better chance to score an ace or cause a poor return.

If you find a serve that your opponent has difficulty returning, continue serving it until the game ends—do not change it. Change your serve only if or when it is not effective. To increase the effectiveness of your serve, vary its speed, direction and height. This will give your opponent more things to consider and worry about while waiting to return the ball.

When serving the ball to your opponent's weak side, you must determine which area on the weak side is the weakest or least effective. You can serve the ball to three different zones on either side of the body. The first zone is the area below the knees called the *low zone.* The *middle zone* is the area between the knees and the shoulders. The *high zone* is the area above the shoulders. For your serve to be most effective, you must determine which of the zones creates the greatest problem of difficulty for your opponent when returning your serve.

If your opponent has trouble retrieving and returning serves below the knees, then send him low, fast power serves or possibly low "Z" serves. (These are even more effective and can be hit with more power when you have a "lively" ball.) When the receiver has difficulty returning serves hit into the middle zone, try either a slow drive, an angle power or a "Z" serve. Receivers who have trouble returning shots above their shoulders should be served lobs.

Another factor to be considered when serving the ball is the type of individual you are playing. If your opponent's style of play is aggressive, slow the game down and hit a variety of slow serves. Conversely, if your opponent is overweight or slow, hit more power serves. The main objective is to alter his style of play, disturb his rhythm and thus reduce the effectiveness of his shots.

Never hit slow serves to an inexperienced and less skilled player. Instead, hit power serves and make him move. Inexperienced players like to see slow serves because they do not react as quickly as more experienced players and they will find your power serves unnerving.

Whichever serve you decide to use, try to hit it as accurately as possible and move as quickly as you can from the service zone to the center-court position. This will put you in a good spot to retrieve the ball should it be returned. To allow you to get to center-court and to enable you to hit a variety of serves, serve the ball from a position near the center of the service zone. This will allow you to move to the center-court area in the least amount of time because you have the shortest distance to cover.

Before serving, consider all these factors. Then utilize them to the best of your ability.

RECEIVING IN SINGLES

In singles, the receiver must assume a position which allows maneuverability to cover the receiving area and protect against all of the various serves. For most players, this receiving position is in the middle of the court and about 3 to 5 feet from the back wall (Illus. 108). The distance from the back wall can be determined by touching the wall with your racquet and stepping forward until your racquet barely touches the wall. This will ensure that you will be able to take a full swing with the racquet without hitting the back wall. This deep court position is also advisable because it is easier to run forward than backward to retrieve a ball.

It is important to assume this court position or one similar to it. If you fail to do this and over-position yourself to one side of the court to protect against a particular weakness, you will create another area for your opponent to attack. A good server will notice this and hit the ball to the unprotected area of the court. This should be avoided if possible.

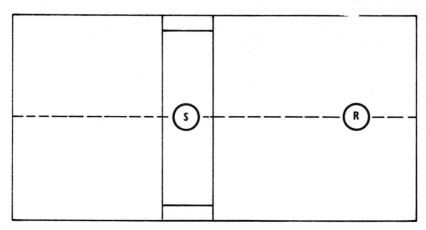

Illus. 108. Center-court receiving position in singles.

A modification of this center-court receiving position is to play slightly off-center favoring your backhand side (Illus. 109). This will allow you to protect your backhand and still utilize your forehand to the fullest. However, if you assume this position you must always be aware that you will have a larger area of the court to cover with the forehand and must be quick enough to run across the court to retrieve the low power serve to that side.

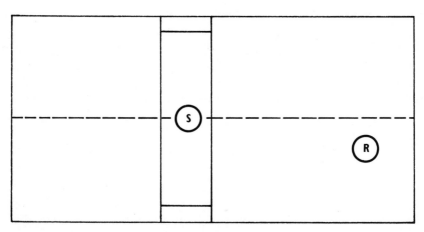

Illus. 109. Off-center receiving position.

TACTICS DURING THE RALLY IN SINGLES

The strategy in singles competition is relatively simple. The primary objective is to hit the ball away from your opponent to an unprotected area of the court, forcing him to run after the ball to retrieve it. This gives your opponent less time to set up and execute the return, thus keeping him on the defensive. When a player continually moves after the ball and does not get ample time to get set before his shot, there is a greater possibility that the return will be weaker than if he was already in position to hit it. Also, the constant running will cause your opponent to fatigue more rapidly during the game, in turn affecting his shot performance. As a player tires, the accuracy of his shots will diminish.

A good rule of thumb is to never let your opponent get set to make a shot—always keep him on the move. This can be accomplished by mixing your shots and the speed and direction in which the ball travels. If you do this, you will keep your opponent worried and guessing where the ball will be hit next.

The shot you use during a rally will depend on both your own and your opponent's position on the court. A guideline to follow is to hit kill shots when your opponent is in back of you, passes if your opponent is to one side and defensive shots if your opponent is in front of you occupying the center-court area.

As soon as you hit a shot, especially from backcourt, move immediately to center-court. Try to maintain and control play from this position. The player who controls this position usually wins the point and the game.

The main reason for hitting a kill shot from the front-court area is that you have an unobstructed view of the ball and you are close to the front wall. This increases your success ratio in performing this shot. Your opponent, on the other hand, must maneuver around you to make the retrieve. To retrieve a well-placed kill shot, your opponent must anticipate correctly and make the commitment of running to it early. When this happens, you can change your shot and hit a pass, catching your opponent out of position and moving in the wrong direction. This is why it is imperative to move to gain control of center-court (Illus. 112).

When your opponent is to one side or if you are in the backcourt and you want to hit an offensive shot, try a pass. This shot allows you more room for error and it forces your opponent to move laterally or even deeper into the court to return the ball, permitting you to move

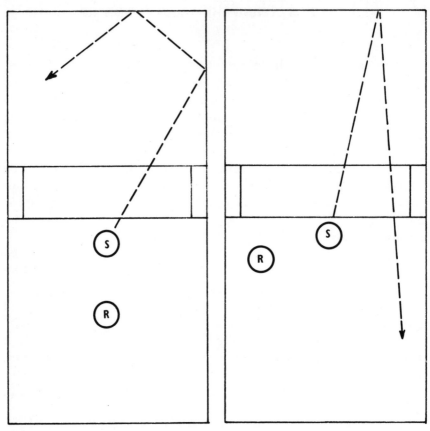

Illus. 110 and 111. Your objective in singles is to hit the ball away from your opponent to an unprotected area of the court.

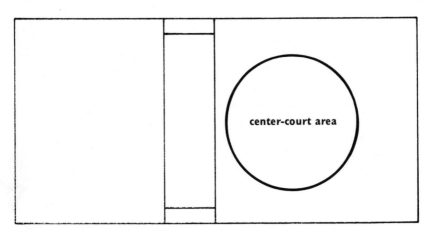

Illus. 112. The center-court area.

to the center-court position. If you cannot hit a pass, then hit a defensive shot to move your opponent from the center-court area.

Prior to playing your match, you should design an intelligent plan of attack. Do not enter the court without specific objectives in mind. If you do not have a sound game plan in mind, then you reduce your chances of succeeding. Knowing of an opponent's weaknesses and aiming your strengths to attack them will help make it easier for you to succeed.

Doubles Strategy

The game of doubles, which requires two players on each side (Illus. 113), is another popular form of racquetball play. It provides some excellent features not found in singles. The game is faster, with more shots being played. The shots must be more accurate than in singles because the greater number of players gives each a smaller area of the court to cover. This game also allows people to play competitively against players who are more highly skilled or in better physical condition, players they would not ordinarily play in singles. The game is less demanding physically because of the smaller area that each player is responsible for covering.

The psychology of doubles play is also quite different from singles.

Illus. 113. The game of doubles requires close teamwork and presents a different kind of challenge from singles.

In singles you are the sole master of your destiny while in doubles you must always consider and often rely on your partner. Teamwork is essential to successful doubles play. Many times team members that work together and complement each other's skills defeat teams comprised of better singles players.

Although many players, especially younger ones, scoff at the idea of playing doubles because of the limited area of play for each participant, it is fun and challenging. In order to win, you must think ahead and hit accurate shots. You have to avoid costly errors because there are two players on the opposing team ready to capitalize on your mistakes. You have to plan and execute your strategy carefully and take fewer chances than in singles.

SELECTING A PARTNER

Before playing doubles—especially in tournament competition—your first task is to find the right partner. This is a lot harder than it may seem. You must find a player who is compatible with your skills and style of play. It also means finding someone you can communicate with and relate to.

For example, if you are right-handed, try to find a left-handed partner to play the left side of the court. This would be ideal. However, there are not enough left-handed players around for every right-hander playing the game. Should you not be fortunate enough to team up with a lefty, your next step is to find someone to protect or compensate for your weaknesses. If you are slow or have a weak backhand, this means finding a player who is fast and has a strong backhand.

The important thing is to analyze yourself and be aware of your strengths and weaknesses. Then try to find a player who can offset your weaknesses without creating any new ones. When this happens, you will have a strong doubles team. The key is the correct assessment of your skills and the selection of a player to supplement them.

Once you choose your partner, practice and play together as often as possible to learn to employ your strategy and iron out any difficulties that may arise during play. This will enable you to understand each other better and to move more efficiently and effectively on the court.

SERVING THE BALL IN DOUBLES

As in singles, serving is an important factor in successful doubles play. Unlike singles, however, it is essential not only to serve the ball effectively but also to let your partner know what type of serve you will use. Knowing which serve will be performed will enable both of you to move quickly to a good defensive position to await the return. Before serving, signal your partner as to which serve you will perform. This will give him a slight advantage over the receiving team, letting him know what to expect.

After the ball is served and passes the short line, both partners on the serving team move back just behind the short line on their respective sides of the court (Illus. 114). (The position assumed will depend on the doubles formation preferred by the team.) This will enable the flow of play to be controlled. It gives you the chance to retrieve shots hit low on the front wall, yet provides enough time to get to balls hit deep in the court. The most important thing to re-

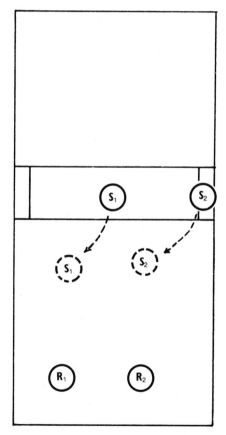

Illus. 114.

member is that you must get to this defensive position as quickly as possible after the ball passes the short line, otherwise you will be caught out of position and your opponents may win the serve. Ideally, the serve should give you enough time to get into good defensive position.

There are several serves that can be used in doubles play. The type of serve will depend upon your team's abilities and your opponents' strengths and weaknesses. Usually, serve most often to the weaker player since your chances of eliciting a weak return are greater. But it's a good idea to occasionally serve the ball to the stronger partner. This will not only keep the team from overplaying a part of the court, but it may even result in a hurried and weak return.

Almost all of the various racquetball serves, if hit accurately, can be used effectively in doubles play. The key is accuracy. A poor serve will move you or your partner out of a good defensive position. One of the most effective and safest serves to hit in doubles is the "Z" serve. When hit to the opposing team's weaker player, it will make your opponents play the ball with one of the weaker shots in their repertoire. It is a very good serve to start a game with because you can put the ball into play in a difficult position with power and not worry about the ball rebounding off the back wall for an easy set-up.

Power or drive serves are only good if they hug the wall or if the receiver has a weak backhand. They must be hit with power and accuracy to be effective or else your opponent will be able to make an offensive return. Lob serves can be effective if they are hit high and deep either near or barely touching a side wall so they die in the backcourt. These should be used only as changes of pace unless you find your opponent has difficulty in returning them effectively.

In summary, whatever serve you attempt, make sure your partner is aware of it. This will enable both of you to move quickly into position for the return.

RECEIVING IN DOUBLES

Teamwork is a very important factor in receiving the serve in doubles. It is essential that each player know his partner's abilities and weaknesses. This will help in determining the receiving position and court coverage for the serve.

While waiting to receive, both partners generally position themselves about 3 to 5 feet from the rear wall (Illus. 115). They stand near the side walls approximately a racquet swing away. From this position, each partner will be able to protect against low power serves hit near the side wall on his side of the court. It also allows him to spin or pivot if necessary to hit balls coming around the corner.

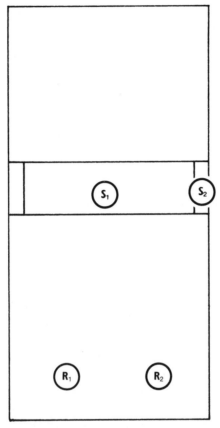

Illus. 115.

On serves that are either hit down the middle or rebound toward the center of the court, it is extremely important to know which of the partners will attempt the return. Knowing the responsibilities and court coverage in this situation is crucial. If you do not know who is going to return the shots down the middle, you will either both attempt to return the shot and possibly collide, or let the ball drop because each of you thought the other was going to hit it. Knowing who will return the serve during play comes with practice, experience and an understanding of each partner's abilities.

RETURNING THE SERVE IN DOUBLES

This is a vital phase of doubles play. It is essential to return the ball effectively because your team is already at a disadvantage—in a defensive position deep in the court. If you do not return the ball effectively, your opponents will have an opportunity to hit an offensive shot and probably score a point.

Returning the serve in doubles requires teamwork. It involves two phases—one partner returning the ball and the other moving into position for the rally. It is crucial to know which of the partners will return the ball. If they do not have confidence in each other, both of them will try to return the ball, back up the other player, or just stand by and expect the other to hit the ball. In any event, it spells disaster for the team.

When both players move to hit the return simultaneously, a collision may be imminent. At any rate, both will be out of position to retrieve the next shot. If either player merely stands and watches or tries to back the other up, then both will be out of position to return the next shot. It is very important for the player not returning the ball to move to a center-court position on his side of the court. This way, he is in a good defensive position to cover the front-court area on both sides if necessary. He also prevents one opponent from getting to a good court position and places that opponent at a disadvantage, especially if the ball is hit to that side. Moving without hitting the ball, then, is important because it allows one of the partners to be in a good defensive position in case the return is poor, and it prevents one member of the serving team from assuming a good position on the court to await the return of the serve.

The second phase is the actual return of the serve. The effectiveness of your service return will determine whether or not your team can be aggressive, take the initiative, and play offensively, or be forced to play defensively from a poor position deep in the court.

Any of the various shots discussed in Chapter 7 can be effective in doubles. The key is to use the right return at the right time. Remember that a weak serve demands an aggressive return using one of the kill or pass shots. An excellent shot to hit is a pass which angles and strikes the side wall at a spot near or just behind where your opponent was standing in the doubles service box. A shot such as this often catches your opponent by surprise. He cannot react quickly enough and the shot has an excellent chance of being successful. The ball either passes your opponent for a winner or jams him, forcing a weak return.

When a good serve is executed and you are not in position to return it offensively, then *don't*. Shoot a defensive shot to the ceiling and try to neutralize the effectiveness of the serve. If you attempt an unwise shot and do not hit it perfectly, then both you and your partner are vulnerable to the return. Always think before you hit. Try to imagine how your return will affect both you and your partner's position on the court. Do not attempt to hit a service return that will compromise either of your positions. Always try to return the ball so your team will either win the serve or be able to move into a good offensive position on the court.

DOUBLE TACTICS DURING PLAY

Teamwork and communication between partners are vital components of successful doubles play. These include everything from pre-game planning to playing the match. Predetermining court areas and responsibilities and knowing your partner's abilities in advance will make your play and court coverage easier. For effective teamwork, each player must know which shots to hit, which ones to let go, and the strengths and weaknesses of his partner. This can only be developed through practice and play.

For a doubles team to be effective, it must control the front-court position. The primary advantage of this position is that it allows the team commanding it to be more offense-minded. The players up front have a better view of the ball and their shots will be more accurate because they are closer to the front wall. The team in the backcourt is at a disadvantage because the front-court players may obstruct their vision for a split second or so. This visual obstruction is not usually a cause for a hinder; however, it can upset a player's timing and cause him to miss the shot or make a weak return. It is also more difficult to hit shots accurately from the backcourt. The doubles team in the backcourt is generally relegated to playing defensively.

All of the shots used in singles can be effectively utilized in doubles play, although some are more effective than others. For example, when you find your opponents lagging back in a defensive position, try a corner kill shot. Hitting the kill so it rebounds to an open area of the court will make it extremely successful. On the other hand, if your opponents play too far forward, then a crosscourt pass will be effective. It is also very wise to cut the ball off on the volley or bounce when the ball is below your waist. This will allow you to hit a more offensive shot because your opponents are behind you. Shots rebounding above your waist should not be played from the front court area. Let them pass and play the rebound off the back wall. You will have more time to get into position to hit an easier offensive shot.

Racquetball shots are even more effective when used in sequence. Do not get into a set pattern of always playing the same shot. Mix them up and keep your opponents guessing.

Another good rule of thumb to follow is to always attack the weakest player of the team. This means that the majority of serves and shots should be directed to this player. By hitting the shots to the weaker of the two opponents, you will have a better chance of forcing an error. Occasionally, change tactics and hit the ball to the stronger player. This will keep him from overprotecting or backing up his partner by overplaying a section of the court. You may also find that if this player is out of position you will win the rally easily by hitting the ball to the unprotected area of the court.

Doubles players should always communicate with each other during a rally and between serves. During the rally, they must constantly let each other know which one of the two will hit the ball. The conversation should be clear and concise, limited to single-syllable words like "mine" or "yours." Trying to communicate with sentences such as "I've got it" or "You take it" are often too long and cumbersome—the rally may also be too fast for you to say more than one word.

It's also good to encourage each other. You can usually do this when the ball is dead and there is a break in the action. Statements like "nice going," "good shot," "good play," or the like can go a long way in letting your partner know that you have confidence in him. It can even destroy the confidence and concentration of your opponents.

In addition to the above tactics, try to control the tempo of play—try to play at the pace you are normally accustomed to playing. If you generally play fast, then try to keep the game moving at a fast tempo. This may be enough to throw your opponents off-balance and enable you to score points quickly before they realize what has happened. On the other hand, if you prefer to play at a slower pace, make sure that you do not let the other team hurry you. Try to slow the game down. Hit ceiling balls and defensive shots until you are in a really good position to hit an offensive shot. Take your time when serving and use your time outs wisely. Remember, you have 10 seconds in which to serve the ball, and you have three time outs per game, each 30 seconds in duration.

When playing doubles, the members of the team generally allocate zones or territories that each will be responsible for covering on the court. This is done by dividing the court into sections with an imaginary line. A clear-cut court division enables a team to set up and devise an intelligent formula for play. There are several systems of dividing court responsibilities and coverage.

The system of doubles play that a team selects will depend on the strengths and weaknesses of both partners. Whatever formation you decide to use, you must work together if you want to be successful. Teamwork is a prime ingredient for successful doubles play. Knowing where your partner is and what your partner can do helps in assigning court coverage responsibilities, which in turn will allow your team to play more efficiently and effectively.

There are four formations or systems of play utilized to cover the court in doubles. They are the side-by-side, the diagonal or modified side-by-side, the "I", or front-and-back formation, and rotation, which is a combination of all the different formations.

SIDE-BY-SIDE

The side-by-side formation is the most frequently used method of covering the court in doubles. It is easy to learn and play because each partner has very clearly defined court coverage and responsibilities. In this system of play, the court is divided into two equal parts by an imaginary line extending the length of the floor from the front to the back wall.

When both players are right-handed, this line is usually moved further to the right (Illus. 116). The side-by-side coverage is no longer 50–50, but 60–40. The partner on the left side of the court assumes the additional responsibility of returning all balls hit down the center of the court. This allows the doubles team to protect the largest portion of the court with their forehands, which in most cases is the dominant stroke.

If one of the players is left-handed, then an almost 50–50 coverage can be played with both partners protecting the major passing lanes near the side walls with their forehands (Illus. 117). In this system, the left-handed player covers the left side of the court, and the right-handed player the right side. Prior to play, you and your partner must decide which of you will cover the shots hit down the middle of the court. The obvious solution is for the partner with the best backhand or the player in the best position to make the return to take the down-the-middle shots. This sounds good in theory; however, if this righty-lefty duo is very good, then the major portion of the shots

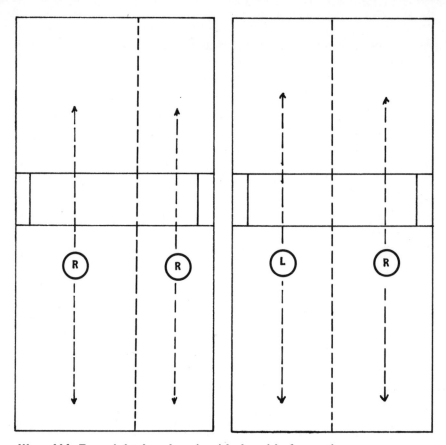

Illus. 116. Two right-handers in side-by-side formation.
Illus. 117. Left-hander and right-hander in side-by-side formation.

will always be returned with a forehand stroke. Most often, it is the left-handed player who has the responsibility of returning the balls hit down the middle because most shots are hit to the left side of the court during play, and a left-handed player can return these shots with a forehand stroke.

The side-by-side formation is excellent for beginning players to use because it gives them the opportunity to use all of the shots of the game. It also teaches them to run forward and backward on the court and return to a good defensive position after hitting.

DIAGONALS

Diagonals is a modified side-by-side system of play used frequently when both partners are right-handed. In this system, the court is divided by an imaginary line extending either from or near the left front corner of the court to or near the back right corner of the court (Illus. 118 and 119). The exact division of the court will depend upon each player's skills and abilities.

Usually, the player on the right side has the major responsibility of covering and protecting the right front corner of the court. He should be a good retriever and have excellent reflexes and racquet control as well as the ability to hit shots that will set up his partner.

The person on the left side is generally the player who has the better backhand and is the better conditioned of the two. He is responsible for protecting the backhand side and returning shots hit off the back wall. To be in a better position to accomplish this, he stands deeper in the court, hence the diagonal look of the formation. This type of formation uses the full potential of each player to the best advantage for court coverage and play.

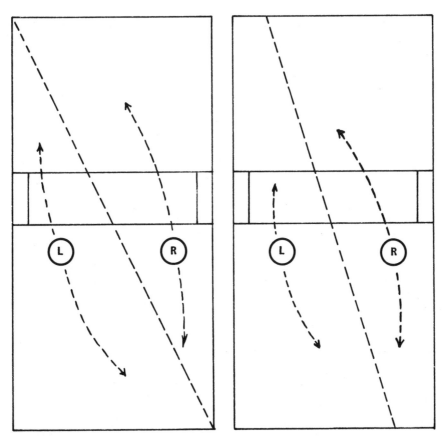

Illus. 118 and 119. Divisions of the court in diagonals.

"I" FORMATION

The "I" or front-and-back formation is rarely used. Although it makes use of the specific abilities of each partner, it does restrict them to specialized play.

In this formation, one player is responsible for the front-court area, while the other player is positioned deep in the court and must cover the backcourt (Illus. 120). To be successful, the front player must be aggressive and quick to retrieve all low shots hit to the front wall, while the backcourt player must be in good physical condition to retrieve the pass shots, play the ceiling ball, and be able to return shots rebounding from the back wall.

The major weakness of this system is the poor defensive alignment of the players. A good pair of opponents can play havoc with this formation by consistently hitting pass shots and forcing the back player to run from side to side with the front-court player unable to help. Sooner or later, the backcourt player will be worn down and execute a weak return. It is also possible for the front-court player to either obstruct the vision of his backcourt teammate by attempting to retrieve a shot, or even get hit with the ball on the return shot. Another obvious weakness is the difficulty of finding two players who possess the unique qualities needed to utilize this formation successfully.

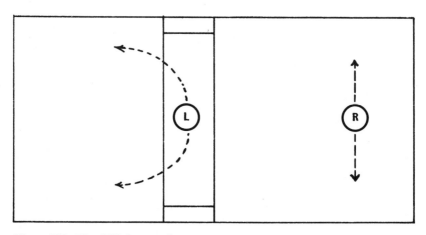

Illus. 120. The "I" formation.

ROTATION

The rotation system is used by advanced players. It is a combination of the three formations previously explained. This system utilizes all the strengths of each formation while eliminating almost all the weaknesses.

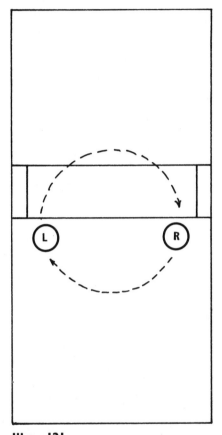

Illus. 121.

When partners have equal abilities, they can use this system to their advantage. Knowing what each other can do, they can move or rotate on the court according to what the situation dictates. It does not matter if they change positions on the court because they know that they each have the ability to play either side of the court.

When playing this style of play, the team generally starts in a side-by-side formation to receive the serve. Depending on the return, they either move to a side-by-side defensive position or a diagonal one (Illus. 121). As play continues, it is possible that one of the players might have to retrieve a shot in the front-court area and move out of position. The doubles team might then be aligned in an "I" formation.

The team stays in this "I" formation until a shot comes at them that will allow them to move back to a stronger defensive position without compromising their play. The rotation or movement of the players is then initiated by the player closest to the front wall who may move in any direction. His partner must move in the opposite direction. Movement by a player to retrieve a shot out of position is the signal for the other partner to rotate to be able to cover the area his teammate has vacated. The players rotate back to their original positions and responsibilities as soon as possible because they are more familiar with them. The team will be stronger because of it.

9. Practice Drills and Tips

After you have learned the proper techniques of hitting the ball, the next step is to practice to gain proficiency in them. Perfecting the racquetball strokes and shots requires hard work, patience, concentration and plenty of practice. An excellent way to develop these skills is the use of repetitive drills. No amount of mental understanding or analysis of the various racquetball skills can be substituted for the actual performance of them. Even a great tactician cannot be successful if he cannot control the ball. Correctly hitting the ball repeatedly until you can perform the shot automatically will help improve your performance. Strokes and shots should be practiced until the racquet feels like a natural extension of your hand. Only when you can execute the strokes and shots with ease will you be able to successfully employ different tactics and strategies in a match.

You can practice the different strokes, shots and the footwork employed in a racquetball match either by yourself or with a partner. Regardless, you should have specific goals and objectives in mind when you practice. Setting up and following a detailed program will help you to use your practice sessions wisely with a minimal waste of time. To help achieve the best results, first attempt to learn and master the easier skills and techniques, progressively working toward the more difficult ones.

Various racquetball practice drills and tips follow. When performing them, concentrate on hitting the ball correctly and accurately. Perform the skills over and over again until they become second nature to you. Hit the ball as if you were actually playing a match. This will help to make your practice sessions more meaningful and alleviate some of the monotony and boredom associated with drilling. How quickly you improve will depend on the amount of time and work that you put into it. Remember, whatever you put into it is what you'll get out of it.

Individual Drills

THE FOREHAND OR BACKHAND RALLY DRILL

Purpose: To improve your strokes, timing and judgment in moving to and hitting the ball. When performed over a long period of time, it will also help to strengthen your arm and grip.

Procedure:

1. To start the drill, assume a forehand hitting stance in the middle of the court in back of the short line.

2. Drop the ball from approximately waist height near the front foot.

3. Hit the ball after it bounces to about waist height so it contacts the front wall at a similar height.

4. As the ball rebounds from the front wall, move into position and hit it on the first bounce.

5. Keep hitting the ball as long as possible using the same stroke.

Tips: Once you master the forehand, follow the same procedure and perform this drill using only the backhand stroke. Start the drill from deep in the court. As you develop more skill, move closer to the front wall to quicken the pace. Also vary your speed and see how many strokes you can execute in a minute.

THE ALTERNATE RALLY DRILL

Purpose: Similar to the Forehand or Backhand Rally Drill. It also accustoms you to changing your grip.

Procedure:

1. Follow the first three steps of the Forehand or Backhand Rally Drill using a forehand stroke.

2. As the ball rebounds from the front wall, move into position and hit it using a backhand stroke.

3. Continue hitting the ball as long as possible, alternating your strokes.

Tips: When doing this drill, start slowly and pay careful attention to both your footwork and grip, and use only the front wall. As your proficiency increases, hit the ball harder, move closer to the front wall and bring the side walls into play. Also vary the speed of the ball.

THE VOLLEY DRILL

Purpose: To improve your reflexes and timing.

Procedure:

1. The drill is similar to the rally drill except the ball is always hit on the fly.

2. Follow the same procedure outline for the Forehand or Backhand Rally Drill.

Tips: First, perform this drill using only a forehand stroke and the front wall. Then execute it using only the backhand. As your skill increases, move closer to the short line and alternate your strokes. This increases the tempo of play and helps to sharpen your reflexes.

THE CEILING BALL RALLY

Purpose: To increase your proficiency in hitting a ceiling ball.

Procedure:

1. To begin, position yourself in the center of the backcourt about 5 feet from the rear wall.

2. Bounce the ball on the floor so it rebounds high above your head.

3. Using an overhand stroke, hit the ball so that it contacts the ceiling and then the front wall.

4. As the ball rebounds from the front wall and traverses the court, move into position to hit it.

5. Return the ball back to the ceiling and keep returning it in this manner as long as you can.

Tips: After you learn to hit the ceiling ball on the forehand side, then practice hitting it from the backhand side. Try to master this stroke until you can eventually hit the ball consistently using alternate strokes. When performing the drill, concentrate and watch where the ball strikes the ceiling in order for it to be a difficult return. Then try to hit that spot. Also vary your angle to the ceiling so you can learn to hit the ball near the side walls.

THE ALLEY PASS DRILL

Purpose: To improve your proficiency in executing the alley pass shot. Use this drill in conjunction with the next two, the angle and the crosscourt drills to perfect all of the pass shots.

Procedure:

1. Assume a hitting stance at the short line and to one side of the court.

2. Toss the ball underhand to the front wall at about shoulder height or softly to the side wall approximately thigh-high (Illus. 122).

3. After the ball rebounds and bounces on the floor, strike it when it is about waist-high (Illus. 123 and 124).

4. Hit it back to the front wall at such an angle that the rebound travels the length of the court in a straight line down the alley of the court (Illus. 125).

Tips: At first, hit the ball softly from the forecourt area watching both the spot it strikes the front wall and the direction of the rebound. As you improve your skill, you should gradually move deeper into the court to execute the shot. Practice from both the forehand and backhand sides.

Illus. 122. Toss the ball underhand to the side wall at about shoulder height.

Illus. 123. As the ball rebounds and bounces on the floor . . .

Illus. 124. . . . strike it when it is about waist-high. Then . . .

Illus. 125. . . . hit the ball to the front wall.

THE ANGLE PASS DRILL

Procedure:

1. Follow the first three steps outlined for the Alley Pass Drill.

2. Hit the ball in such a manner that it will strike the front wall and angle low and fast directly to the side wall without hitting the floor. The ball should hit the side wall near the short line.

Tips: The ball should be hit forcefully and low. A ball that is hit too high will rebound off the back wall for an easy set-up. This drill can be practiced more effectively with another player. When working with a partner, position him in the court near where you want the ball to hit the side wall. Practice this drill using both the forehand and backhand strokes.

THE CROSS COURT PASS DRILL

Procedure:

1. The first three steps are the same as those used in performing the Alley Pass Drill.

2. The ball is then returned either on a fly or after it bounces, directly to the front wall so it angles to the opposite side of the court.

Tips: Practice this shot initially from the front-court area. As your accuracy improves, move deeper into the court. Perform this drill using both the forehand and backhand strokes.

THE KILL SHOT DRILL

Purpose: To improve your accuracy and execution of the different types of kill shots—the straight kill, the corner kill, and the fly kill.

Procedure:

1. Position yourself in the front-court area in a good hitting stance.

2. Toss the ball underhand about waist-high or lower to the front or side wall (Illus. 126).

3. After the ball rebounds from the wall, let it bounce on the floor (Illus. 127).

4. Wait until the ball drops to below knee level before attempting one of the kill shots (Illus. 128-131).

Tips: First learn to hit the straight kill, next the corner kills and then the fly kills. When practicing the fly kill, set yourself up by throwing the ball high on the front wall to give you time to get into position to hit it. If you use the side wall, toss the ball so it bounces before hitting it, then contact the ball after it rebounds from it. Make sure you try to wait until the ball is below your knees before attempting to hit any of the kill shots. This will help your accuracy, which in turn will make the shot successful. Practice this drill until you can hit the kill shots from either the forehand or backhand side. You must have this shot in your repertoire to compete against highly skilled players.

Illus. 126, 127. In the kill shot drill, toss the ball underhand at about waist height . . . let it bounce on the floor.

Illus. 128, 129, 130 and 131. Wait until the ball drops to below knee level before attempting one of the kill shots.

THE BACK WALL DRILL

Purpose: To improve your timing and footwork in hitting the ball after it rebounds from the back wall.

Procedure:

1. Assume a position deep in the middle of the court about 3 to 5 feet from the back wall.

2. Toss the ball with an underhand motion softly to the back wall.

3. After it bounces on the floor, adjust your steps and time your stroke so that you will hit the ball as low as possible to the front wall. (The ball should be hit below knee level.)

Tips: Practice this drill initially by trying to catch the ball as low as possible. After you can do this successfully, try the actual shot. You should practice the proper footwork diligently until you can perform it instinctively. Next, vary the speed and height of the ball toss. This will give you more practice in moving to and hitting the ball. After you have acquired some skill, try tossing the ball so it bounces before hitting the back wall. Then try to hit the ball after it rebounds from the back wall and before it strikes the floor. Always try to hit the ball as low as possible when performing this drill.

THE SERVICE DRILL

Purpose: To improve your skill and accuracy in the various racquetball serves.

Procedure:

1. Position yourself in the middle of the service zone.

2. Execute any of the various serves.

3. Hit the same serve repeatedly until you can execute it consistently.

4. Repeat the same serve a minimum of 25 times.

Tips: Learn to hit all of the basic racquetball serves—do not rely on just one particular serve. When practicing the serve, watch the spot where the ball strikes the front wall and the flight of the rebound. Once you determine the spot and the angle you must hit to perform the serve successfully, keep practicing until you can hit it consistently. After you have acquired some skill and accuracy in executing the serve, then find another player and practice the Serve and Return Drill (page 134).

THE SIDE-SHUFFLE

Purpose: To improve a player's efficiency to get to the ball. Besides running, there are three other methods that can be used—the side-shuffle, the crossover step and the oblique running.

Procedure:

1. Stand in the middle of the court in the racquetball ready position.

2. Using sliding movements, move to one side, touch the wall, and return to the starting position.

3. Move to the opposite side, touch the wall, and return.

4. When moving to the right:
   a. First move the right foot to that side.
   b. Transfer your body weight to this foot.
   c. Pick up the left foot and slide it next to the right one.
   d. Continue this movement until you reach your destination.
   e. Reverse this procedure when moving to the left.

Tips: Moving two or three steps in either direction is sufficient. Remember, after touching the side wall return to the center of the court. Also use this drill in combination with the other footwork drills.

THE CROSSOVER STEP

Procedure:

1. Stand in a ready position at the center of the court.

2. Pivot on the right foot.

3. As you pivot, bring the left foot in front and across your body stepping toward an imaginary ball.

4. Swing your racquet as if to hit a shot.

5. Reverse this procedure when going to the left.

Tips: Practice moving the racquet behind your body at the same time as you pivot. This will save you time in preparing to hit the oncoming ball. Combine this drill with the other footwork drills.

OBLIQUE RUNNING

Procedure:

1. Assume a ready position about 5 feet behind the short line in the middle of the court.

2. Then run and touch the right or left corner of the front wall and return to the starting position.

3. When running to the right corner, try to stop near the corner with the left foot forward; then play a shot.

4. Reverse this foot procedure when going to the left corner.

Tips: A variation of the drill is running to the rear corners of the court. If you move to the right side, pivot on the right foot. Then, using a crossover step, start running to the corner. When you get near the corner, plant your right foot and step toward the front wall with the left foot and swing. Then return to the original starting position. Do the reverse when going to the left. This drill can also be utilized with the other footwork drills.

Two-Player Drills

THE CROSSCOURT RALLY DRILL

Purpose: To practice and improve both the forehand and backhand strokes under game-like conditions.

Procedure:

1. Both players assume positions about 10 to 15 feet behind the short line and on opposite sides of the court.

2. Play is initiated by one player bouncing the ball and then hitting it to the front wall so that it angles to the opposite side of the court for the other player to hit.

3. The ball is then returned in a similar manner.

4. The ball is continuously hit back and forth as long as the ball is in play.

Tips: Try to keep rallying the ball as long as possible. Initially, only use the front wall. Then bring the other walls into play, varying the height, speed and direction of the ball. In order to practice both the forehand and backhand strokes equally, players reverse positions on the court and perform the same drill.

THE SERVE AND RETURN DRILL

Purpose: To increase your skill and proficiency in both serving and returning the serve.

Procedure:

1. One player (the server) takes up a position in the middle of the service zone while the other player assumes a receiving position in the middle of the court about 3 to 5 feet from the back wall.

2. The server then practices any one of the various serves over and over again while the receiver works on returning it.

3. After a number of serves (at least 20), the receiver and server change positions.

Tips: The server should concentrate on trying to keep the ball deep and off the back wall. The receiver should attempt to hit an outright winner on a weak serve or a neutralizing shot on an effective serve.

THE CEILING RALLY DRILL

Purpose: To improve the execution of the ceiling shot.

Procedure: The procedure is the same as the Crosscourt Rally Drill except the ball is hit alternately to the ceiling.

Tips: Vary the speed and angle of hitting the ball. Try to keep the ball deep and near a side wall. Also keep it from rebounding off the back wall. Then reverse sides so you can practice both the forehand and backhand ceiling shots equally.

THE SET-UP AND SHOT DRILL

Purpose: To improve your shot execution under simulated game situations.

Procedure:

1. One player assumes a position in the front-court while the other stands in the backcourt.

2. The player in the front-court hits the ball in such a way as to set the ball up for the backcourt player to hit.

3. The backcourt player watches the path of the ball and then moves into position to execute the shot being practiced.

Tips: Utilize this routine to practice all the racquetball shots. When moving to hit the ball, have in mind the shot that you are going to perform. Do this sequence several times in succession. After you have acquired a degree of skill, then work on another shot. Reverse positions after a sequence of shots so your partner will also have an opportunity to practice.

THE POINT-SCORING DRILL

Purpose: To practice the serves and shots under game-like conditions.

Procedure:

1. One player puts the ball in play by serving.

2. The other player returns it.

3. The ball is then rallied alternately using the various strokes and shots until one of the players fails to make a legal return.

Tips: The serve can either be played alternately, or the server can continue to serve until he loses it. If one player dominates the serve, then by mutual agreement each player should serve a designated number of times. No score is kept.

10. Safety and Etiquette

Safety

Racquetball is a sport where risk of serious injury is minimal compared to many other sports—very few injuries occur during play. Except for minor muscle aches and pains, rarely does a racquetball player fracture a bone, dislocate a joint, or experience a serious muscle pull. Of the injuries that do occur, however, there is a high potential for eye injuries and injuries associated with being hit with a racquet. These injuries can usually be minimized or avoided when proper safety precautions are taken.

Too frequently, people learn to play racquetball from a friend, who in turn learned from another friend, and so on. Although they learn how to hit the ball and enjoy doing it, they often do not learn the safety practices that will help them avoid injury and make their game safer and more enjoyable.

To help decrease the potential for injury to yourself or your opponent, use the safety equipment previously described and adhere to the following guidelines.

SAFETY GUIDELINES

- Play and abide by the rules of play.

- Stay in good physical condition.

- Warm up properly before play and warm down after play.

- Be courteous and adhere to court etiquette.

- Wear the proper clothing.

- Use the proper safety equipment.

Above all, use your head and follow good safety practices. To even further reduce the incidence of court injuries there are several other practices that each player should know and understand.

Never play with a wet ball. A wet ball has a tendency to slide and bounce unnaturally. It is very difficult to control and can very easily result in a misdirected shot which could hit your opponent. Dry the ball as soon as possible after the rally.

Replace wet clothing. When your clothing has become saturated with perspiration, you should change it. If you do not, it will no longer absorb your sweat and the excess will drip to the floor making it slippery and dangerous to run on.

Wipe the floor dry when wet. Should the floor become wet from your clothing or from diving on the floor to retrieve a shot, dry it immediately after the rally.

Towel off. If you do not have a chance to change into dry clothing right away, or even after you have changed your clothes, dry yourself with a towel. Toweling without changing is only a temporary preventive measure, and you should be aware that moisture will still drip to the floor.

Control your emotions. Do not lose your cool on the court. You can injure yourself quite easily by swinging the racquet and striking the wall. You can also cause injury by hitting an unsuspecting opponent with the ball or even your racquet.

Do not hit a fault or out serve. If the serve is not a legal one, do not play it. The server, realizing it is not legal, may relax and turn around to get the ball. If you attempt to return the ball you may strike him.

Tie your shoelaces. Laces that are not tied are dangerous. You can step on them running to hit a shot and cause injury to yourself or your opponent.

Secure your glasses. Glasses not safely fastened could fall to the floor and break, making another potentially dangerous situation.

Do not push or bump your opponent. Racquetball is a non-contact sport. The rules do not permit this, and you can cause an injury doing it.

Avoid overswinging. An excessive follow-through can hit and injure an unsuspecting player who is concentrating on retrieving the ball.

Do not crowd your opponent. Playing too close to your opponent puts you in a very vulnerable position and increases your chances of being hit with the racquet.

Know your opponent's swing. Knowing how your opponent swings the racquet will enable you to pick your position on the court in relation to his racquet swing. This is known as "racquet awareness." This knowledge may prevent you from being hit with the racquet.

Control your swing when hitting balls near the wall. When a ball is hit near a side wall, do not swing as forcefully as you would if it were away from the wall. If you swing forcefully and do not judge your swing correctly, you might strike the wall. This can result in a broken racquet, finger, wrist, arm, or possibly a dislocated shoulder.

Always watch the ball. By watching the ball, you can move out of position to keep from being hit by the racquet or the ball.

Protect your eyes. When watching the ball, you should take certain precautions to protect your eyes. This can be done in several

Illus. 132 and 133. Protect your eyes by placing your racquet in front of your face.

ways. You can use your racquet as a protective device by placing it in front of your face. Hold it firmly and let it rest on your shoulder (Illus. 132 and 133) or the force of the ball will drive it into your body producing a "waffle face." Or you can use your arms for protection. Raise your arm to protect your face and barely peek over it

Illus. 134 and 135. You can also raise your arms to protect your face.

(Illus. 134 and 135). This enables you to duck your head quickly and protect your eyes should the ball come in that direction.

If you follow these rules and use the proper safety equipment, you will significantly reduce your chances of being injured on the court.

Racquetball Etiquette

In order to insure that the game of racquetball will be enjoyable for all participants there is a basic standard to which each and every player should adhere. This is simply the appreciation and employment of good sportsmanship throughout the entire match. Although this concept is not unique to racquetball, it is extremely important because of the close quarters and intimacy of play. Also, the majority of racquetball contests are played on an informal or recreational basis without the services of a referee. When playing a contest without an official, it is even more important that all rules of sportsmanship be upheld or the game could deteriorate to something other than racquetball and diminish the enjoyment of play.

Sportmanship in racquetball can be defined as the unwritten rules of the game and the way players should conduct themselves throughout the match. Simply speaking, racquetball involves consideration and courtesy for others.

During a racquetball match, any form of unsportsmanlike conduct, such as screening, blocking, or shoving, should not be tolerated. Instead, players should try their best to win using their own skill within the rules of play. Only by winning in this manner will a player have a worthwhile feeling of accomplishment.

Listed below are some of Do's and Don'ts, or the "unwritten" rules of racquetball play.

DO

• Introduce yourself to your opponent prior to play if you have not already met.

• Avoid unnecessary conversation during and between rallies.

• Announce the score before serving, stating the server's score first.

• Apologize if you hit your opponent with the ball or racquet.

• Compliment your opponent when he makes a good play.

• Replay all questionable calls.

• Call illegal hits you make during play.

• Dry the ball if it becomes wet and let your opponent examine it before continuing play.

• Display good sportsmanship whether you win or lose.

• Congratulate or thank your opponent either for winning or playing the match.

- Play doubles instead of singles when others are waiting to play.

- Thank the referee for officiating at the conclusion of the match.

- Accept your opponent's decision when he calls a hinder.

- Give your honest opinion when a question arises during play.

- Maintain a spirit of fairness throughout the match and it will usually be reciprocated.

DON'T

- Show up late for a scheduled match.

- Enter a court until a rally has ended.

- Make excessive noise when your opponent is hitting the ball.

- Interfere intentionally with your opponent's shots.

- Hit your opponent deliberately with the ball or racquet.

- Serve until your opponent is ready.

- Push or crowd your opponent.

- Use obscene language on the court.

- Criticize your partner.

- "Hog" or overplay the court in doubles.

- Lose your self-control on the court.

11. Conditioning for Play

Getting in Shape

Competitive racquetball is a game of skill where shot selection, placement and execution far outweigh a player's need for muscular strength. At the same time, it is also a game of concentration and endurance for which muscular strength and stamina, as well as general cardio-respiratory endurance, are essential. In other words, racquetball has both skill and physical fitness components.

For you to be at the peak of your game, both of these components should be at a high level simultaneously. If you compromise either of them, your game will suffer. For example, when you experience fatigue during play, your concentration and shot execution will be more adversely affected if you are in poor condition. Or if you are in good physical condition but unable to execute certain shots because of lack of skill, then you will still have little or no success during play. Therefore, it is important to work on and improve whichever component is lagging at any given time.

You can improve your fitness component along with your skill component by playing more. The fitness component, however, can also be improved through running or other training methods, while it is unlikely that your skill component can be improved without practice.

CARDIO-RESPIRATORY FITNESS

An excellent method for improving your cardio-respiratory fitness is to jog or run for a minimum of 20 minutes to a maximum of one hour several times a week. During this running period, you will probably run between 2 or 3 miles in a 20-minute period or 5 to 7 miles in a one-hour period. Long-distance running will help you to develop the stamina that is so necessary when playing a long three-game match. This type of running will also help to improve the muscular condition and endurance of your legs. Other ways to improve your cardio-respiratory fitness are interval running, jumping rope, and bicycle riding.

Interval running consists of running short sprints followed by fast walks for equal or long distances. It is used to help develop cardio-respiratory fitness through the manipulation of several variables, these including the distance covered, the speed or pace at which it is covered, the number of times it is performed, and the amount of rest between each run. By keeping one or more of these variables constant and systematically varying the remaining ones, you will create an overload on your muscles and thus improve your fitness. In addition to improving your stamina, interval running will also help to increase your speed on the court.

Jumping rope and long-distance bike riding are two other exercises that improve your stamina. Both of these will also help to condition your leg muscles, which are vital for good racquetball play.

MUSCULAR FITNESS

Along with cardio-respiratory fitness, improved muscular strength and endurance will also enhance your overall court performance. As previously stated, when your muscular fitness is deficient, you will note a gradual decline in your skill performance, continuing until the match ends. Therefore, it is important to develop a high degree of muscular fitness.

The muscles that should be developed and conditioned for playing racquetball are those which are primarily used in running to and hitting the ball. These include the muscles of the legs, lower back, and the racquet arm. Development of these muscles will also help to prevent or minimize injury in addition to helping you move more quickly on the court and hit with greater power.

Calisthenics and weight training exercises can be used to improve muscle strength. They should be dynamic, progressive in resistance or repetitions, and should mimic the actions of the muscles during play. They should include stretching exercises together with the strength exercises to help offset the potentially harmful effects of excessive strain to muscles, tendons and ligaments. This means the potential for injury in any situation will be reduced because the tissues are both more resistant and compliant.

Calisthenics used for stretching and improving flexibility fall into two major categories, each of which has some theoretical relevance to racquetball players. The two types are ballistic and static exercises. Ballistic stretching means bouncing or stretching to the constraining limits of a joint and repeatedly going beyond it. On the other hand, static stretching is accomplished beyond it and holding that position for 6 to 10 seconds. Of the two methods, static exercises are considered safer while ballistic stretching more closely imitates the actions that occur during strenuous play and may therefore produce better protective adaptations.

No attempt will be made to outline all of the many calisthenics and weight training exercises that a racquetball player can perform during a workout. There are too many different exercises that can be beneficial, and the type and amount of exercise that an individual should do will vary from person to person depending upon the desired objective.

Before playing racquetball or beginning a physical fitness training program, consult your physician and have a complete medical exam. Then meet with a physical education specialist to help you set up a program of exercises. By consulting professionals, you will minimize the risk of harming yourself by vigorous exercise or incorrect programming and maximize the effects of training. After that, the rest is up to you.

Warm-Up

Prior to playing or working out, you must warm up your muscles properly. To "warm up" is to engage in a series of light exercises designed to loosen the muscles and tendons and increase the circulation of blood and oxygen prior to strenuous exercise or competition. More specifically, a proper warm-up will result in:

- increased range of movement (more flexibility)

- increased muscle efficiency and performance

- increased muscular power

- prevention of muscle soreness

- prevention of muscle injury

- less strain on the heart—your most important muscle.

When warming up, follow a program of exercise that will involve the entire body, especially those areas that will be utilized in the more vigorous workout or play. The warm-up period should allow your body to gradually move from a state of inactivity to one of more vigorous activity. Start the warm-up period slowly and increase the pace and intensity of the exercises until your body begins to feel loose and warm. Perspiration is a good indicator that the muscles of your body are warm and ready to engage in more intensive exercise.

After you have progressively loosened and warmed up the muscles and tendons of your body, you are ready to play racquetball or start your workout. Remember that the amount of time spent warming up will vary with each individual. You will have to assess your own capacity to warm up. Generally, your warm-up period should last about 10 to 15 minutes and serve as an introduction to more strenuous exercise and play.

To allow yourself adequate time to warm up, arrive early for your match and do the stretching exercises either in the locker room or outside the court. Inside the court, run in place or jog for about 1 to 2 minutes and then practice hitting most of the shots you will use during the match. Start slowly at first and increase your tempo in hitting the shots. The exercises can be utilized in warming up your body for more vigorous exercise and racquetball play.

The Toe Pointer: Sit on heels with the toes and ankles stretched backward. Both hands are placed on the floor behind the hips. The body weight is balanced over them (Illus. 136). Just sitting in this position will stretch your leg muscles.

Illus. 136. The toe pointer.

The Calf Stretcher: Assume a standing position about 2 to 3 feet from a wall, then place your hands on the wall about chest-high. While the heels of your feet are touching the floor, bend your elbows until your chest touches the wall (Illus. 137).

**Illus. 137.
The calf stretcher.**

The Hamstring Stretch: Assume a sitting position with the legs extended and the toes pointing toward your head. Then lean forward placing your hands first on your shins, then your ankles, and finally your toes (Illus. 138).

The Lower Back Stretcher: Assume a prone position on the floor, then grasp your ankles from behind. Hold this position for about 5 seconds (Illus. 139).

Trunk Twister: Sit on the floor with legs extended. Then turn at the trunk and cross leg and hand over so leg and both hands are on the same side. Keep the head in the direction of the trunk. Repeat this exercise on the other side (Illus. 140).

146

**Illus. 138.
The
hamstring
stretch.**

**Illus. 139.
The lower
back
stretcher.**

**Illus. 140.
The trunk
twister.**

Upper Trunk Stretcher: Assume a prone position on the floor and place your hands in a push-up position several inches in front of your shoulders. While keeping your pelvis touching the floor, extend your arms so your chest is raised from the floor (Illus. 141).

Illus. 141. The upper trunk stretcher.

Upper Back Stretcher: Assume a prone position on the floor. Then raise your legs until they are over your head and parallel to the floor. After several tries, raise your legs until they touch the floor. Your hands and arms should remain in contact with the floor during the exercise (Illus. 142).

Illus. 142. The upper back stretcher.

The Shoulder Stretch: While in a standing position, raise your right arm over your right shoulder. At the same time place your left arm behind your back and raise it to meet the right hand. Try to hook or touch your fingers (Illus. 143 and 144). Then repeat the exercise on the opposite side.

Illus. 143 and 144. The shoulder stretch.

The Inner Thigh Stretch: Lie on your side and raise the upper leg as high as possible. Hold this position for about 5 seconds, then repeat on the other side (Illus. 145).

149

Illus. 145. The inner thigh stretch.

Warm-Down

It is just as important to include a warm-down period in your exercise program as it is to include a warm-up. To warm down means to do a series of light exercises that allows you to taper off from strenuous activity.

During the vigorous activity of a racquetball game, the muscles assist the circulation of blood. When this activity stops abruptly, its effect could result in pooling of blood in the extremities which might cause muscle cramps, muscle spasms, or even a sudden black-out. This is why you should gradually change the tempo of your activity when you conclude play. By slowing the pace down naturally, you allow the body to cool down.

After the match has ended, alternately walk and jog slowly for a brief period of about 5 to 10 minutes. This will give your body adequate time to cool down.

12. Analyzing Your Play

Before you can hope to significantly improve your play, you must first have a good idea of which areas of your game need help. The first step, then, is to analyze your game, and there are a number of ways to do this.

One method is to analyze and evaluate your court performance during play using the evaluative tools in this section. This will enable you to better understand your shot pattern and accuracy as well as your overall method of play.

A second method is to test yourself periodically. By utilizing skills tests, you will be able to determine your skill proficiency and measure your improvement. Besides these tests, you should also test your intellectual knowledge of the game. A written or oral examination will make you aware of how much you really know about racquetball. Then you can take the necessary steps to acquire more knowledge. The more you know and understand about the game, the better you will like and appreciate it.

The final method of analyzing your play is your performance in tournament competition. This will give you an indication as to how you compare with other players either locally, regionally or nationally, depending on the tournament you enter.

Once you have located the areas in which you are deficient, the next step is to work on improving them. To accomplish this, you need to practice. The use of repetitive drills is an excellent method to improve your skills. Chapter 9 deals with drills and exercises that can help you to improve your play.

After you analyze and evaluate your play, devise a systematic plan to improve your weaknesses and maintain your strengths. Do not neglect practicing your strengths while improving your weaknesses, and conversely, do not neglect weaknesses by spending too much time practicing your strengths.

Scorecard Analysis

The main purpose of the racquetball scorecard is to record the points that each player makes during a game. However, with a little ingenuity, it can be transformed to serve another function. It can be developed into a tool that can be used to evaluate a player's performance. Although this tool provides only limited information, it does provide additional insight as to a player's court performance.

To prepare the scorecard to collect data for analysis, you must divide it into periods called *innings*. An inning is a round of play during which each side has an opportunity to serve. A *half-inning* allows only one side the opportunity to serve. Draw a box in the upper right corner of each inning of your scorecard. This box is used to record the number of points scored during that inning. The illustration below is an example of how the scorecard should be drawn. The larger box is used to collect the data and to keep a running total of the score for the game in progress.

Contestants	Innings									Total

COLLECTING THE DATA

First secure the services of a friend who understands the game and show him how to record the data.

To complete the scorecard, your friend simply places a dot in the larger area of the half-inning for each point that is scored. After the server loses the serve, the dots are counted and the total is recorded in the box in the upper right corner. The number recorded in this box is referred to as the *inning score*. The inning scores are added to keep a *running score,* recorded in the large area of each box. This procedure is followed for both contestants until the game is finished.

INTERPRETING THE DATA

After collecting the data, the next step is to analyze it. The information that the scorecard provides shows the consistency of your play.

If the scorecard reveals that a player scores points almost every inning with very few scoreless innings, you can infer that he concentrates while serving, is very skillful, plays consistently and is probably in good physical condition.

When an individual's play is sporadic or inconsistent, there will be several innings in succession at different intervals when he doesn't score. If this happens, you can conclude the following:

1. The player does not warm up properly or is a slow starter if he suffers scoreless innings at the onset of the match or beginning of each game.

2. The player does not have the skill to perform consistently.

3. The player does not have the physical stamina or strength to play consistently over an extended period of time.

4. The player does not have the stamina or lacks the "killer instinct" to finish a match when he is unable to score toward the end of the contest.

Having this knowledge about yourself or your opponent is very beneficial. It can serve as a device to plan your practice sessions and game play and to improve your pattern of scoring. It can also serve as an incentive to devise a game plan to attack your opponent by playing harder during the times when your opponent's scoring declines occur.

Below is an example of a hypothetical match. It indicates that Jack is a fast starter while Ron is obviously a slow starter. It also indicates Ron's inability to score consistently. In other words, Ron is probably a streak player. When he's hot, he really plays well. If you were playing against him, it would be in your best interest to call a timeout during his scoring periods to try and cool him off. This inconsistency of play, however, will probably cause Ron to lose many matches. Through practice, Ron's play can be improved and he can become more than just a streak player.

Having factual evidence about your own and opponent's play will enable you to plan intelligently both your practice sessions and your game plan. It will help you to become more quickly aware of your own and your opponent's strengths and weaknesses. It is important to note that the data from one scorecard is inconclusive. A series of scorecards will provide more reliable and valid data about you and your opponent. If used with other methods of evaluation, the racquetball scorecard can be a very valuable asset in improving your play.

Game 1

Contestants	Innings								Total
Ron	0 / 0	0 / 0	· 1 / 1	...4 / 5	0 / 5	0 / 5	::: 7 / 12	1 / 13	13
Jack	....5 / 5	...3 / 8	...3 / 11	0 / 11	...3 / 14	..2 / 16	· 1 / 17	..4 / 21	21

Game 2

Contestants	Innings								Total
Jack	::: 6 / 6	.. 2 / 8	...4 / 12	0 / 12	...3 / 15	· 1 / 16	0 / 16	::: 5 / 21	21
Ron	0 / 0	0 / 0	0 / 0	::: 6 / 6	0 / 6	0 / 6	....8 / 14		14

Shot Analysis and Scouting Chart

The Racquetball Shot Analysis and Scouting Chart is an excellent instrument for gathering factual data pertaining to a player's shot performance while playing a game or match. An analysis of the information collected will provide insight into how a player actually performed.

More detailed than a simple scorecard, this chart can serve a dual role. First, it can be used to provide you with objective data about your own strengths and weaknesses. This knowledge will help in planning your practice sessions more effectively. It may even make you more determined to practice harder and longer to improve your deficiencies.

The second purpose is to gather information about a future opponent. The data you collect, together with your own knowledge of racquetball, will allow you to prepare more thoroughly for your upcoming match. The following information on your opponent's play can be gleaned from this chart.

• The type of offensive shots he relies on most to score points or win the serve.

• The shots he uses infrequently.

• The shots he uses successfully.

• The types of serves he utilizes.

• The number of aces he scores on the serve.

• The number of errors he commits in serving.

The information provided by this chart is more reliable when collected over a period of several games. One game is not conclusive. However, after one match you will begin to see a pattern developing.

COLLECTING THE DATA

Set up the chart as on page 158. Then find a friend and show him how to place the data on the chart. This person should be knowledgeable, or at least familiar, with the rules and skills of racquetball play. If you are scouting an opponent, you can do it yourself.

To record the data, place a dot in the appropriate box opposite the name of the player being observed. All shots that a player employs during a game that score points, win or lose the serve, or are attempted unsuccessfully should be recorded. At the conclusion of the contest, total the dots in each box, then add the totals for each box to the appropriate boxes from other games that have been previously played. After you've done all this, you will be ready to examine and analyze the data.

INTERPRETING THE DATA

Having collected the data, you are now ready to analyze it. The information collected will allow you to easily determine the strengths and weaknesses of the player being evaluated. It will provide information about the shots and serves used during play and the strokes used to perform them.

The chart shows the results of a racquetball match. After

Game I

Contestants	Passes BH	FH	Kills BH	FH	Ceiling BH	FH	2-Ball BH	FH	Serves ACES	OUT	DF'S	Errors BH	FH
Jack	6	7	1	9	4	2	0	2	5	0	0	7	2
Ron	4	3	5	7	6	1	0	0	0	1	4	3	8

Game 2

Contestants	Passes BH	FH	Kills BH	FH	Ceiling BH	FH	2-Ball BH	FH	Serves ACES	OUT	DF'S	Errors BH	FH
Jack	9	8	4	10	5	1	0	1	4	0	0	8	1
Ron	6	2	6	8	5	2	1	0	1	0	3	2	9

Match total

Contestants	Passes BH	FH	Kills BH	FH	Ceiling BH	FH	2-Ball BH	FH	Serves ACES	OUT	DF'S	Errors BH	FH
Jack	15	15	5	19	9	3	0	3	9	0	0	15	3
Ron	10	5	11	15	11	3	1	0	1	1	7	5	17

examining this chart, you will notice that each player has several weaknesses and strengths. The statistics reveal that both players are falling into a set pattern of play. It appears that the players usually hit percentage shots, such as the pass or ceiling, with their weaker strokes. They also seem to be more aggressive and offensive-minded when using their dominant strokes.

The data reveals that Jack has a weak backhand while Ron has a strong backhand and a weak forehand. It also indicates that Ron needs to practice his forehand accuracy because of the number of errors he committed while executing it. If Ron does not improve his kill shot success ratio, then he will have to avoid using this shot. On the other hand, Jack's kill shot accuracy on the forehand side is excellent.

The chart also shows that Jack has a very formidable serve, indicated by the number of aces he scored. Conversely, Ron should practice his serve to avoid the unnecessary double faults he committed.

Finally, from this chart, you can see the strength of each player's serve. As mentioned previously, Ron needs to concentrate more when serving to eliminate the number of mistakes he made. There were far too many service errors.

Once you determine your opponent's style of play, it will be easier to devise a plan of attack. If you were to play either of these players, you could concentrate your attack on their weaknesses when serving and hitting the ball. Further, since you know your opponent's shot preference, it will be easier for you to anticipate your opponent's shots and position yourself to retrieve them.

For example, when you hit the ball to the weak side, you can move to a position deeper in the court because it is likely that your opponent will hit a defensive shot that will travel to that area. Likewise, if you hit the ball to your opponent's strong side, you can move closer to the front wall since a kill shot is likely.

Contestants		Jack Serving		Ron Receiving		Ron Serving		Jack Receiving	
BH = Backhand FH = Forehand		BH	FH	BH	FH	BH	FH	BH	FH
Ace Serves	Power (straight)								
	Power (Angle)								
	Lob								
	"Z"								
	Slow Drive								
"Out" Serves									
Double Faults									
Pass Shots	Alley or Wall								
	Angle								
	Cross court								
Kill Shots	Straight								
	Outside - Inside								
	Inside - Outside								
Drop Shot									
Ceiling Ball									
Z - Ball									
Lob									
Around - the - Wall									
Errors									
Pass Shots	Alley or Wall	B A C K W A L L S H O T S							
	Angle								
	Cross court								
Kill Shots	Straight								
	Outside - Inside								
	Inside - Outside								
Errors									
Hinders	Unintentional								
	Avoidable								
Game No. Tournament:									
Date Recorder									

Shot analysis and scouting chart.

THE DETAILED CHART

The chart just discussed is a valuable tool for objectively analyzing racquetball play. It is simple to prepare and use. As you learn more about racquetball and how to use this chart, you can devise a chart that is more complex, depending on the type of information you want to obtain. After you compile and analyze the statistics, it will be up to you to put the information to good use.

Skills Testing

The use of skills tests is another way to measure a player's progress. By utilizing skills tests, players can chart their progress in improving a particular skill. As you improve your skills, you will also start to notice improvement in your overall play. Do not be discouraged if your skills are improving and you are still losing contests. The most important thing to remember is that you are getting better. Eventually you will achieve success.

The following tests can be employed to measure your skills. In addition, they are good practice routines. When testing, make sure you perform them at regularly scheduled intervals. If you perform them in this manner, you will have a standard from which you can compare and measure your progress.

THE RALLY TEST

This test is used to measure racquet control. Test yourself for three periods, each lasting 30 or 60 seconds. Whichever time you choose, keep it consistent each time you test yourself.

To start, take up a position in the middle of the court, behind the short line. Bounce the ball, hit it to the front wall, and, as it comes back to you, hit it again. Continue rallying against the front wall using forehand and backhand strokes until the time limit is up. Score a point for each shot that is hit from behind the short line and hits the front wall before it hits the floor. In other words, you score one point for each good racquetball shot, as long as you hit it from behind the short line. The clock is started simultaneous with the first contact of the racquet and ball.

Test yourself for three periods and average the scores. This test, as the others which follow, may not tell you very much about your game the first time you try it. However, if you test yourself periodically, you will get a good idea as to how you are progressing and how quickly your game is improving.

THE FOREHAND OR BACKHAND RALLY TEST

As the name implies, this is really two different tests. The objective is to isolate and test either the forehand or backhand stroke. The procedure is the same as the rally test, except that you use only one stroke in each test. Its main purpose is to measure racquet control and proficiency.

THE POWER TEST

This is a test both of strength and control. Divide the court into six areas, five on the actual court and the sixth being the rear wall (Illus. 146). Then put a line about 4 feet off the floor on the front wall—this designates the area under which the ball must strike the front wall.

To start the test, stand behind the short line and toss the ball about shoulder high to the front wall. As the ball rebounds from the wall, let it bounce once and hit it (you must be behind the service line) so that it strikes the front wall below the 4-foot line. If the ball hits above the line, you score zero; if it hits below the line, you score points depending upon which numbered zone the ball then lands in. Score 1 point if it lands in zone one, 2 points if it lands in zone two,

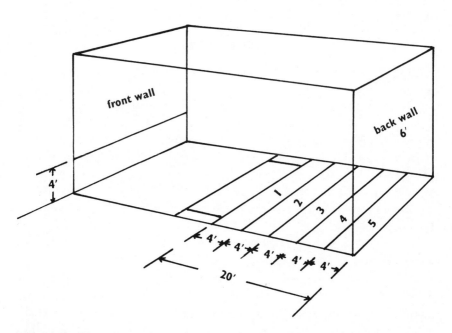

Illus. 146. Division of the court in the power test.

and so on, up to 6 points if it reaches the back wall without bouncing on the floor. Try this for three sets of ten attempts using only forehand strokes, then three more sets with backhand strokes.

Tournament Test

A good measure of a player's ability is his actual performance under pressure in tournament play. Regardless of how high you score on skills or knowledge tests, performance in tournaments is probably the best indication of your ability.

Although there are many different types of tournament structures, the round robin is the best way to measure a player's performance in relation to the other players in the tournament. It is more reliable to judge a player's ability when using round-robin play as a measuring device because in this type of tournament each contestant is given the opportunity to play against all the other contestants.

On the other hand, the single elimination tournament is probably the least valid as a measure of ability—the best player does not always win. There are too many intangibles involved. This tournament is not a good gauge of skill because a player can lose only once before being eliminated from further play. Thus, it is possible for the better players to lose because of an off day in the early rounds of play.

The round-robin tournament eliminates the majority of these extraneous factors, allowing the better player to finish higher in the standings.

Knowledge Testing

Knowledge and understanding of racquetball concepts are two important factors that lead to a better appreciation of the game for the player as well as the spectator. It is essential to acquire knowledge of the techniques, strategy, and rules of play. This will make it easier for the player to play and more enjoyable for the spectator to watch. The following list of thought-provoking questions will help you to test your knowledge of the game. If you've read this book carefully, you should have no trouble answering them.

1. What are the agencies that govern racquetball play?

2. What are some of the benefits derived from playing racquetball?

3. Describe the different types of courts on which you can play racquetball.

4. What type of clothes can be worn to play racquetball during informal play? During formal or tournament play?

5. Explain the requirements for selecting a ball for play.

6. What are some of the factors that should be considered in selecting and purchasing a racquet?

7. List and explain the functions of the safety equipment used in racquetball.

8. Explain how to grip a racquet properly for the forehand stroke. The backhand stroke. The overhand stroke. The underhand stroke.

9. Explain the basic procedure used to execute a forehand. A backhand. An overhand. An underhand.

10. What is meant by footwork? Explain how it is used.

11. What is a legal serve? An out serve? A fault serve? A dead ball serve?

12. Name and describe the basic racquetball serves.

13. Explain the court position you should be at when receiving a serve in singles. In doubles.

14. Explain the advantages and disadvantages of the different shots used to return the serve.

15. List the shots used in play. Which are offensive? Which are defensive? How do you execute them?

16. Why is it important to warm up before playing a game?

17. Describe a good warm-up routine.

18. Why and how should a player warm down after playing a match?

19. How does conditioning affect a racquetball player's performance?

20. Explain how to set up a racquetball conditioning program.

21. What is meant by flexibility exercises? Explain.

22. What is meant by anticipation?

23. What does percentage play mean?

24. Describe a basic singles strategy that can be employed in a game.

25. What are the different types of formations used in doubles play? Explain the advantages and disadvantages of each.

26. Name and explain the different methods that can be used to evaluate racquetball performance.

27. What is meant by court etiquette?

28. List and explain the safety practices that should be followed when playing racquetball.

29. How many points must be scored to win a game? A match? Who can score points?

30. What is a hinder? An avoidable hinder?

31. How many time outs can a player take during a game?

32. Name and describe some of the drills that can be used to improve a player's skill.

33. Explain the following terms: Inning. Half-inning. Game. Match.

34. What is meant by side out? Hand out?

35. Diagram a racquetball court. Note the dimensions and explain the markings on the court.

GLOSSARY

ace: A legal service that completely eludes a receiver and results in a point for the server.

alley: The area on both sides of the court that is formed by an imaginary line extending from the doubles service box to the front and rear walls. It is 18 inches wide and 40 feet long.

angle serve: A power serve that angles low to the side wall without touching the floor and then bounces in the service court before striking the back wall.

anticipation: The ability to predict and move into position to return an opponent's forthcoming shot.

around-the-wall-shot: A shot in which the ball strikes three walls. The ball hits the side wall first, the front wall, and then the opposite side wall.

avoidable hinder: An intentional interference of an opponent's shot resulting in an "out" or a "point" depending upon whether the player committing the offense was serving or receiving.

backcourt: The court area extending from the short line to the back wall.

backhand: The stroke used to hit the ball with the arm across the body and the back of the hand facing the direction of the swing.

backhand grip: The method of grasping the racquet when executing a backhand shot or stroke. Also called the "palms down" grip.

backspin: Spin imparted on the ball causing it to rotate in the direction opposite to which the ball is travelling. Also called "bottom spin."

backswing: The part of the stroke in which the racquet is moved to a position behind the body to prepare for the forward swing to contact the ball.

back wall: The rear wall of the court. It must be a minimum of 12 feet high.

back wall shot: A shot made from the rebound of the ball off the rear wall.

block: The act of preventing an opponent from either seeing, hitting, or moving to the ball with some part of your body.

body contact: Physical contact that interferes with an opponent retrieving or returning a ball.

bottom board: An imaginary area on the front wall near the floor that is 2 inches high and extends the width of the wall. Kill shots are directed to this area.

bottom spin: See *backspin.*

bumper guard: A protective covering on the rim of the racquet head.

ceiling ball: See ceiling shot.

ceiling serve: Any served ball that contacts the ceiling after striking the front wall. A fault serve.

ceiling shot: A ball that is hit against the ceiling either before or after striking the front wall. The ball then bounces high off the floor to a spot in deep court.

center-court control: Maintaining the center-court position during the course of a rally while keeping an opponent deep in the court.

center-court position: The middle area of the court located about 3 to 5 feet in back of the short line.

change-of-pace serve: A slow serve hit with less force than normal that is used to change the tempo of play.

change-of-pace shot: An off-speed shot hit with less force than normal to change the tempo of a rally.

chop: To hit the ball with a downward stroke with the racquet facing up to impart backspin on the ball.

control: The ability of a player to hit the ball to a designated spot.

court: The area of play for racquetball.

court hinder: Interference by an obstacle on the court that deflects the ball such as a latch, light fixture, etc. The point is replayed.

crosscourt shot: A ball hit diagonally from one side of the court to the other side.

crotch: The juncture or crack where two playing surfaces meet.

crotch ball: Any ball that hits the juncture where two playing surfaces meet.

crotch serve: Any served ball that strikes the juncture of two playing surfaces. It results in an out serve.

crowding: Standing or playing too close to an opponent.

cutthroat: A game involving three players with the server playing against the other two.

dead ball: Any ball that is not in play.

dead ball hinder: An unintentional hinder that results in the point being replayed.

dead ball serve: A serve that is replayed, but does not result in any penalty nor cancel a previous illegal serve.

default: The loss of a match by a player who declines or is unable to play.

defective serve: Any of the three types of illegal serves—dead ball, fault, or out serves.

defensive position: The back area of the court.

defensive shot: Any shot that is utilized to gain resting time or continue a rally rather than end it.

diagonals: A system of doubles play in which the playing responsibilities or court coverage are assigned by dividing the court into two areas with a line extending from the left front corner of the court to the right rear corner of the court.

die: When a ball loses momentum or speed.

dig: To retrieve a low-hit ball which might have ordinarily been a winner.

doubles: A game played by four players with two on each team.

drive serve: See *power serve.*

drive shot: See *pass shot.*

drop shot: A delicately hit ball that hits soft and low on the front wall.

error: Failing to successfully return a reasonably playable ball during a rally.

exchange: See *rally.*

eye guard: A protective device constructed of wire or plastic that is worn over and around the eyes to prevent injury.

fault: An illegal serve or infraction of the service rules.

float: A ball that travels so slowly it seems to hang in the air allowing an opponent enough time to get to it and make the return.

fly kill: Any of the kill shots hit in the air after the ball rebounds from the front wall and before it bounces on the floor.

fly volley: Any ball hit in mid-air after rebounding from the front wall and before bouncing on the floor.

follow-through: The act of continuing the motion or swing after the ball is contacted; the completion of the swing.

foot fault: An illegal serve that is the result of the server or the server's partner leaving the service zone or service box before the served ball passes the short line.

footwork: The manner of moving the feet in coordination with the body to get into position to hit the ball and strike it efficiently.

forehand: A stroke used to hit the ball with the palm of the hand moving in the direction of the swing.

front-and-back formation: A method of doubles play in which a team lines up one in front of the other. The forward player assumes front-court coverage, while the other partner is responsible for covering the backcourt. Also called "I" formation.

front-court: The area of the court extending from the short line to the front wall.

front-wall-side-wall kill shot: A kill shot in which the ball hits the front wall first and then the side wall.

game: Competition played until one player or team scores twenty-one points.

game point: The point, if scored by a player or team, that will decide the winner of the game.

grip: The manner in which the racquet is held or the part of the racquet that is grasped by the hand.

half-and-half formation: See *side-by-side formation.*

half volley: Any ball that is hit on the "short" bounce immediately after striking the floor.

hand out: The loss of service by the first partner of a doubles team.

hinder: Any interference of a player by an opponent during a serve or rally. There are two types—*dead ball hinder* and *avoidable hinder.*

hit: The act of striking the ball with the racquet.

"I" formation: See *front-and-back formation.*

illegal serve: Failure to serve the ball according to the rules of play.

inning: A round of play in which both players or teams have the opportunity to win and lose the serve.

inside-corner kill shot: See *front-wall-side-wall kill shot.*

interference: Obstruction of an opponent's play. See *hinder.*

IRA: The International Racquetball Association; one of the governing bodies of racquetball play.

kill shot: Any ball hit low on the front wall that is either impossible or almost impossible to return.

live ball: Any ball that is in play. Also a ball that bounces too high.

lob serve: A softly hit serve that strikes high on the front wall and travels in a high, floating arc near a side wall to a spot deep in the court.

lob shot: A ball that is hit similar to the lob serve except it is executed during a rally.

long serve: A fault serve that rebounds to the back wall from the front wall without first touching the floor.

match: A racquetball contest of the best two out of three games.

match point: The point, if scored by a player or team, that will decide the winner of the match.

middle-court: The area of the court that extends from the service line to the receiving line.

missed ball: An out serve in which the server swings and misses the ball; results in a loss of serve.

mixed doubles: Doubles competition in which a male and female are paired against another male and female.

NRC: The National Racquetball Club.

non-front wall serve: An out serve in which the ball strikes a surface other than the front wall before hitting the front wall.

offensive position: The strategic area of the court; approximately center-court.

offensive shots: Any of the racquetball shots that are designed to score points and end a rally.

out: Failure to return a ball that is in play. Also see *out serve.*

out-of-court ball: Any ball that leaves the playing area. If the ball hits the front wall first and then leaves the court, the point is replayed. When a ball leaves the playing area without hitting the front wall, then point or loss of serve results against the player who hit the ball.

out-of-court serve: A service fault in which a legally served ball is hit out of the playing area.

out-of-order serve: In doubles play, when either partner serves out of the proper serving order; results in an out serve.

out serve: An illegally served ball that results in a loss of serve.

outside-corner kill shot. See *side-wall-front-wall kill shot.*

overhand shot: A shot that is used to hit the ball when it is over a player's head.

pass shot: A ball hit hard and fast so it rebounds out of an opponent's reach.

point: The unit of scoring in racquetball; any serve or rally won by the player or team serving.

point of contact: The spot where the racquet meets the ball.

power serve: A served ball that rebounds low and fast from the front wall to a rear corner of the court.

rally: The play that takes place after a legal service until a player or team fails to return the ball.

ranking: The rating of players on a list according to their ability based on performance in recent tournaments.

ready position: The stance a player assumes while waiting to return a serve or shot during play.

receiver: The player or team not serving.

receiving line: The imaginary line 5 feet in back of the short line indicated by a 3-inch vertical line on each side wall. The player or team waiting to receive the serve must stand behind this line until the ball is served.

receiving zone: The area of the court extending from the receiving line to the back wall.

referee: The individual who makes all judgments in accordance with the rules during a match.

rest period: The intervals of time in which a player or team may rest according to the rules of play.

rollout: A kill shot hit so low that it does not bounce off the floor but rolls along it.

rotation: A method of doubles play which involves incorporating a combination of all other methods of doubles play.

screen ball: A ball that rebounds close to a player, either during a serve or rally, obstructing an opponent's view of the ball.

semi-kill shot: A poorly-executed kill shot that rebounds high enough off the floor for an opponent to retrieve it.

serve: The manner of putting the ball into play.

server: The player who serves or puts the ball into play.

service box: The area on either side of the service zone where the non-serving partner of a doubles team must stand until the ball is served and passes the short line.

service line: The front boundary line of the service zone which is located 5 feet in front of and parallel to the short line.

service zone: The area of the court located between the outer edges of the short and service lines where a player stands to serve.

serving side: The player in singles or the team in doubles serving the ball.

set-up: A weak return of a shot that results in an easy opportunity for an opponent to hit a shot for a winner. Also called a *plum ball*.

shadow ball: See *screen ball*.

shoot: The attempt by a player to hit a kill shot.

shooter: A player who relies heavily on the use of the kill shot.

short ball: See *short serve*.

short line: The back boundary of the service zone. It is 5 feet in back of and parallel to the service line. The short line also divides the court into two equal parts.

short serve: A fault serve where the ball rebounds from the front wall and either bounces on or in front of the short line.

side-by-side formation: A system of doubles play in which the playing responsibilities and court coverage are assigned by dividing the court into two equal areas with a line extending down the middle of the court from the front wall to the back wall. Each partner is responsible for the balls hit on his side of the court.

side out: Loss of serve by a player or team.

side-wall-front-wall kill shot: A kill shot hit so the ball strikes the side wall first and then the front wall. Also called an *outside-corner kill shot*.

singles: A game played between two players.

skip ball: Any ball that hits the floor just prior to striking the front wall.

straddle ball: A ball that passes between the legs of a player who has just returned the ball.

straight kill shot: A kill shot that hits the front wall directly and rebounds in the same direction from which it came.

thong: The strap attached to the handle of the racquet and worn around a player's wrist.

three-quarters one-quarter: See *diagonals*.

three-wall serve: See *two-side serve*.

three-wall shot: See *"'Z" ball.*

top spin: Spin imparted on the ball causing it to rotate in the direction it is travelling in.

touched serve: An out serve in which the served ball, on the rebound from the front wall, touches the server or the server's partner on the fly while any part of the partner's body is out of the service box.

tournament play: Formally organized competition.

two-side serve: A fault serve in which the served ball hits three walls on the fly before hitting the floor.

unavoidable hinder: See *hinder.*

undercut: To impart backspin on the ball.

U.S.R.A.: The United States Racquetball Association; one of the governing bodies of racquetball play.

volley: See *fly volley.*

wall ball: A ball hit so that it travels close to or hugs a side wall. Also known as a *wallpaper ball.*

winner: A shot that ends a rally. Often used interchangeably with *kill shot.*

"Z" ball: A defensive shot that hits the front wall, a side wall, and then the opposite side wall before touching the floor.

"Z" serve: A legal serve that strikes the front wall, then a side wall, travels crosscourt bouncing on the floor behind the short line before striking the opposite side wall. After hitting the side wall, the ball rebounds parallel to the back wall.

INDEX